A WORLD BANK COUNTRY STUDY

Economic Growth in the Republic of Yemen
Sources, Constraints, and Potentials

The World Bank
Washington, D.C.

Cover Photos: A man sifting grains through a basket in Yemen; a farmer plowing fields in Yemen. World Bank Photo Library.

ISBN: 0-8213-5210-5
ISSN: 0253-2123

Library of Congress Catologing-in-Publication Data

Economic growth in the Republic of Yemen : sources, constraints, and potentials.
     p. cm. — (World Bank country study)
  Includes bibliographical references.
  ISBN 0-8213-5210-5
  1. Yemen—Economic conditions. 2. Yemen—Economic policy. I. Series.

HC415.34 .E255 2002
338.9533—dc21

2002032188

CONTENTS

Tables, Figures, Boxes and Annexes

ABSTRACT

This country study is based on the findings of several background papers which were undertaken in direct response to the request of the Government of Yemen (GoY) for assistance in studying the sources of economic growth for the preparation of the country's Poverty Reduction Strategy Paper (PRSP). It focuses on the potentials and constraints of the various economic sectors and assesses the business and governance environment in Yemen.

The report is composed of three parts. Part I reviews economic performance in Yemen and assessess the government medium- and long-term development plans. It provides a detailed analysis of the major structural characteristics of the Yemeni economy and the main economic sectors with the aim of identifying their constraints and potentials. It also assesses the impact of economic reforms undertaken in the mid-1990s on the trends and the structure of economic growth. Then the potentials and the constraints of the main economic sectors (agriculture, industry and services) are analyzed with special emphasis on the "potential" and "promising" sectors for the attainment of economic growth targets.

Part II of the Report is devoted to the study of Yemen' private sector environment and external competitiveness given the importance accorded to the private sector and exports in the medium- and long-term development plans. It investigates why private sector's response to stabilization and structural reforms in Yemen has been slow and highlights the results of a survey that was undertaken specifically for this study for about 1,000 private enterprises in five governorates in Yemen in November 2001. It also provides important elements for future reform agenda for developing the private sector and improving governance in Yemen. This part also focuses on external trade and export performance in the 1990s with special emphasis on external competitiveness, which underpins export growth.

Given the policy relevance of the analytical work undertaken for this study, Part III of the Report concludes with policy recommendations including a concise policy matrix for accelerating and sustaining economic growth in Yemen in the medium- and long-terms. The recommended reforms take into consideration the existing potentials and constraints of the main economic sectors, the objectives of the medium- and long-term development plans and the feasibility and sequencing of the policy reforms. This part of the Report is, therefore, intended to provide an input into the PRSP and into deliberations among the Bank, the GoY and stakeholders on future economic reforms in Yemen. The focal point of the report is mainly on the need to improve the governance structure and private sector environment to tap the potentials of the Yemeni economy.

ACKNOWLEDGMENTS

A multi-sectoral World Bank team prepared this report. Led by Nadir Mohammed, the team included Gianni Brizzi (tourism), Jean-François Barrès (agriculture and fisheries), Arup Banerji (governance and private sector), Julia Devlin (private sector), Elisabeth Sherwood, (manufacturing), Masakazu Someya (trade and external competitiveness), Caralee McLiesh (private sector survey), Mohammed Al-Sabbry (research assistance and manufacturing) and Maria Victor Handal, Mary Lou Gomez and Isabelle Chaal (team assistance).

The peer reviewers (M. Ataman Aksoy and Philip E. Keefer) provided valuable comments and suggestions on the first draft of the report. Mustapha Nabli (Chief Economist and Director, MNSED) and Dipak Dasgupta (Sector Manager, MNSED) provided useful insights and suggestions during the various stages of the preparation of the Report. Valuable comments were also received from the IMF Middle Eastern Department (particularly Edward Gardener and Sherwyn Williams) during discussion of the Concept paper and on the first draft of the Report.

The themes researched in this report were identified during a series of consultations with the Yemeni authorities and individuals in 2001. In particular, H.E. Minister Ahmed Mohammed Sofan, Minister of Planning and Development, requested the analysis for preparation of the Poverty Reduction Strategy Paper (PRSP). The team working on the Strategy Vision 2025, the Second Five-Year Plan and PRSP provided guidance on the content of the report. Suggestions and comments by Mr. Abdel Rahman Tarmoum (Vice-Minister of Planning and Development), Dr. Mutahar Al-Abbasi (Deputy-Minister of Planning and Development) and Dr. Yahya Al-Mutawakil (Coordinator, the National PRPS Team) are highly appreciated and acknowledged. Professors Mohammed Al-Hawiri and Abdel Karim Al-Sieyaghi (Sana'a University) participated in the study by organizing and undertaking the private sector survey in 5 Governorates.

Finally, the analysis leading up to this report benefited from many discussions with Sana'a based staff of several external partners and NGOs. Their contributions are gratefully acknowledged.

ABBREVIATIONS AND ACRONYMS

CBY	Central Bank of Yemen
CMSA	Constant Market Share Analysis
CPI	Consumer Price Index
CSO	Central Statistical Organization
DHS	Demographic Household Survey
EPA	Environmental Protection Authority
FDI	Foreign Direct Investment
FFYP	First Five-Year Plan
FTA	Free Trade Area
GDP	Gross Domestic Product
GDI	Gross Domestic Investment
GIA	General Investment Authority
GOAMM	General Organization for Antiquities, Manuscripts and Museums
GOPCH	General Organization for the Protection of Cultural Heritage
GoY	Government of Yemen
ICOR	Incremental Capital Output Ratio
IFC	International Financial Corporation
IMF	International Monetary Fund
ISIC	International Standard Industrial Classification
LDB	Live Data Base (the World Bank)
MENA	Middle East and North Africa
MoF	Ministry of Finance
MoHP	Ministry of Health and Population
MoPD	Ministry of Planning and Development
PDRY	People's Democratic Republic of Yemen
PEC	Public Electricity Corporation
PRSP	Poverty Reduction Strategy Paper
RCA	Revealed Comparative Advantage
REER	Real Effective Exchange Rate
RoY	Republic of Yemen
SFYP	Second Five-Year Plan
SNA	System of National Accounts
TFP	Total Factor Productivity
TFR	Total Fertility Rate
UN	United Nations
US	United States
WHO	World Health Organization
WTO	World Trade Organization
YAR	Yemen Arab Republic
YR	Yemeni Rial

CURRENCY EQUIVALENTS
Currency Unit = Yemeni Rial (YR)
Exchange rate: YR 174.3 YR per 1 US Dollar (as of 4 May 2002)

YEMEN FISCAL YEAR
January 1st – December 31st

EXECUTIVE SUMMARY

Rapid and sustained growth (in excess of 5% per annum) is critical for sustained poverty reduction in Yemen. This has been recognized by the government's second five-year plan (SFYP). The attainment of such target is, however, very challenging and will require extremely aggressive changes in both the overall business environment and the governance structure as well as the elimination of significant obstacles to growth in particular economic sectors.

Unification of Yemen in 1990, subsequent political transformation towards a multi-party system, and building of democratic and civil institutions have put the country on the right track to accelerate economic development and growth.

Economic growth in the 1990s was impressive despite the impact of three major shocks in the early 1990s (drought, the Gulf war, and the civil war). During 1990-2000, real GDP growth averaged 5.5%, which translated into 1.5% increase in GDP per capita due to the high population growth rate. In the early 1990s, the external shocks led to an increase in financial imbalances and the GoY initially resorted to direct controls restricting imports, investments and movements of the exchange and interest rates. In 1995, the GoY embarked on a program for economic reforms and stabilization with the aim of enhancing the foundations of a market-based and private sector-led economy. It focused on stabilization, price and trade liberalization, fiscal adjustments and reform of the exchange rate regime. Partly responding to the strong stabilization and reform outcomes, GDP growth picked up to 6.4% during 1995-2000.

GDP growth in Yemen was, however, driven mainly by factor accumulation (labor and capital) in the 1990s. Productivity growth was negative for most of the decade with only modest improvements after the implementation of economic reforms. This points to the substantial scope for deeper reforms to improve non-oil output.

During implementation of the First Five-Year Plan (1996-2000), the GoY decided to prepare the SFYP within a framework of a long-term strategy. For that purpose, the Strategic Vision 2025 was formulated. It plans for the achievement of an annual average GDP growth of 9% in the coming 25 years, reducing population growth rates and raising productivity. The Vision emphasizes strongly the importance of poverty reduction as well as the creation of a conducive environment for private sector development. As the first plan within that long-term vision, the SFYP was prepared and it targets the achievement of an average GDP growth rate of 5.6% as well as raising the contribution of non-oil sectors in GDP from 71% to 75% by 2005; with an implied average annual growth rate of 8%. Ambitious targets for agriculture (6.7% per annum) and services (8%) were planned while the growth rate of industrial value-added was set at 3.0%.

The achievement of the targets of the SFYP and the long-term vision is a challenging task. Sustained and higher economic growth rates would require major improvements in the business environment and governance structure, enhancement to domestic security, maintenance of macro-economic stability, pursuit of structural reforms to raise productivity, and addressing a number of constrains in the various economic sectors (see sections below). Without addressing these obstacles, the medium and long-term growth targets are unlikely to be met. Furthermore, the investment levels (both private and public) expected by the plan to

1

achieve the GDP growth target appear too high and are inconsistent with expected improvements in the human resources base and productivity increases resulting from perusal of structural reforms.

Economic growth will require significant increases in private investment, particularly in non-oil sectors. Without significant and notable improvements in the governance structure, regulatory environment and in the security situation with which property and contract rights are enforced, this investment is unlikely to be forthcoming.

Evidence suggests the need for improving total factor productivity in the Yemeni economy as an important source of economic growth. One of the primary drivers of productivity improvement and strong growth performance is the capability of firms, which is greatest when operating in a healthy investment climate. Well-functioning private markets are also a powerful way to help the poor catch-up by providing the opportunity to enhance living standards.

Both the Strategic Vision 2025 and the SFYP recognize the pivotal role of the private sector in achieving high and sustained rates of economic growth. They call for strengthening of the partnership between private and public sectors while according the private sector the leading role in realizing economic and social development. The SFYP aims to raise the share of the private sector in total GDP, and in non-oil GDP to 53.7% and 72.3% respectively by 2005. This would require a real growth in private sector output by an average annual rate of 10%.

The Report analyses the private sector environment in Yemen, based on available literature and a private sector survey undertaken specifically for this study. The main findings include the following: (a) private sector firms are languishing in an environment characterized by weak governance and corruption, major administrative obstacles, high taxes and inefficient tax administration and unfair business practices; (b) the majority of firms are small, service-oriented workshops operating in captured domestic markets with few opportunities for profitable expansion; (c) the investment climate is viewed as a high-risk and characterized by lack of a level playing field for foreign and domestic firms; (d) small firms face relatively minimal difficulties in entering a market, but face significant obstacles to growth in value-added and specialization as a result of high levels of risk and uncertainty in the general investment climate, unfair business practices, administrative obstacles and costly and uncompetitive infrastructure services; (e) access to electricity, land and legal services is difficult and costly, together with high transactions costs associated with incidences of crime and theft, insufficient internal transport networks and others; and, (f) larger firms tend to do better because they are able to internalize the risks, in part through conglomeration and building up in-house capacity in critical inputs. Larger firms also tend to benefit from well-entrenched networks of influence as well as access to external markets and finance.

The main challenge for Yemen is then how to attain a dynamic and broad-based growth in the private sector, given its two critical and inter-related factors: (i) the weak institutional environment for the private sector in terms of weak governance and few market-promoting institutions, and (ii) the small size of the manufacturing sector, and the persistently small size of most Yemeni firms. The Report recommends the focus on systemic approaches to issues but also fast track methods for addressing critical bottlenecks while providing important demonstration effects in the short run (enclaves in the form of industrial zones). Priorities for action include putting in order the governance structure, promoting macroeconomic stability and legal certainty, minimizing administrative regulations, addressing corruption and unfair business practices, and improving the quality of infrastructure services mainly by elimination of excessive and arbitrary regulations.

Improving the investment climate will require greater attention to improving the functioning of markets and infrastructure networks. There are three required building blocks in this approach. First, there is a need to strengthen commitment to building an economy based on market disciplines and income incentives through prudent macroeconomic management, open trade policies and a competitive exchange rate. Second, priorities for action also include developing formal market-based institutions including a framework of commercial law and a workable legal system that support market-based transactions. Strengthening of public sector capacity in facilitating business entry and growth and tax administration is also an important component of developing effective agencies and institutions to support the development of a market economy. Third, ensuring competitive access to infrastructure such as electricity, land, water and telecommunications as well as fair competition in product markets is crucial for enhancing the profitable expansion of firms.

Private investment is expected to increase by 21% per annum during the SFYP. This is unlikely to take place without marked improvements in the governance, business and investment environments. Public investments are also planned to increase by 13% per annum during the plan. While there is an envisaged important role for public sector in Yemen during the plan, large fiscal spending may jeopardize the macroeconomic stability hardly achieved in the second half of the 1990s. And while government allocations planned during 2001-2005 accord higher allocations for the social and agricultural sectors, the allocations for transport and communications are projected to decline. This may be inconsistent with the sectoral growth targets of the plan particularly if private sector provision of these services remains weak.

Reliance on domestic demand limits the prospects for faster and sustained GDP growth. Indeed, Yemen's merchandise exports performed considerably better in the late 1990s and have contributed much of the GDP growth. The impact of policy reforms (flexibility of the exchange rate and trade liberalization) made a significant impact on the competitiveness and good performance of exports. Such gains need to be preserved and enhanced further by deeper liberalization and improvements in trade-related infrastructure and services.

Rapid employment-generating economic growth will only be possible if agriculture, fishing, tourism and manufacturing lead the way. Rising domestic security concerns, excessive and arbitrary regulations in infrastructure and services, weak legal and judicial systems, and difficulties in securing land titles hamper output expansion in most of these sectors. In addition, each of these sectors confronts significant challenges that the government must resolve.

Achieving an average growth rate of 6.7% per annum in agricultural output during the SFYP appears to be an ambitious, though achievable, target. The major constraints in the sector include severe water shortages (due to rapid depletion of ground water), vulnerability to fluctuations in rainfall, prevalence of traditional cultivation techniques and rapid expansion in Qat plantation. Water is apparently under-priced and water rights are heavily contested and insecure. Qat, the main cash crop, is certainly damaging to other crops and to water sustainability. Nonetheless, given the substantial yield gap, huge post-harvest losses, value-added of most crops can grow faster than the plan's target if productivity is increased, cultivated area is expanded, Qat plantations are controlled in addition to improvement in irrigation management and extension services. Raising fisheries output by 13% annually could also be realized, as was the case in the FFYP with a high risk of collapse to the stock of fish. The current system of licensing is not based on reliable knowledge of standing stocks and requires the immediate attention of the government.

The SFYP projects an annual increase in industrial output by 3% only, although it predicts very high growth rates for manufacturing, construction and public utilities. The expected low contribution of the sector was based on the assumption of stagnation in oil value-added during 2001-2005. Oil production was the most significant contributor to GDP, economic growth, fiscal revenues, exports and foreign exchange earnings in the 1990s and is expected to decline in the short- and long-terms. Yemen's recoverable oil reserves currently stand at 2.8 billion barrels and unless new oil discoveries are made oil fields are expected to dry up in less than two decades at current production levels. The SFYP projects stagnation in oil value-added throughout 2001-2005 on the assumptions of annual decline in production from producing fields and annual increase from new fields. These estimates, however, need to be revised in the light of new projections of oil production with increased projected production levels during 2001-2003 and sharper declines during 2004-2005. More importantly, although oil is still a dominant sector there is no evidence of a Dutch disease problem but the GoY needs to cater for this expected decline in oil production in its fiscal targets and to ensure continuous reductions in non-oil fiscal deficits.

Yemen's proven gas reserves are about 12-15 trillion cubic feet. Currently only domestic consumption is met and the potentials of gas exports will remain unutilized during the SFYP. The Natural Gas Export project faces many constraints including lack of secured external markets and financial resources necessary for the infrastructure of the projects in addition to strong competition from other countries in the region. Similarly, the country has also huge mining reserves (gold, platinum, titanium, gypsum, etc.). Exploration and production is mainly hampered by security concerns, conflicts over land ownership and poor infrastructure. Both gas and mining resources have great potentials in the medium- and long-run if the constraints facing them are addressed in a comprehensive manner.

Manufacturing sector in Yemen —characterized by high degree of industrial and geographical concentration, family ownership, and low value-added to inputs ratio— remains a small sector in comparison with other similar countries. It contributed only 9% of GDP in the 1990s and its contribution to merchandise exports has been even weaker (less than 1%). The protectionist policies pursued until mid-1990s have contributed to the fragility and inefficiency of the sector. Macroeconomic stability, trade liberalization and reform of the exchange rate regime adopted since mid-1990s started to have a positive impact on manufacturing sector. The plan targets an annual rate of growth of manufacturing value-added of more than 9%. It also seeks to encourage exports of manufactures and to support the development of small-scale industries. The realization of these targets, however, largely depends on removal of the constraints in the sector (access to land, high production costs, poor infrastructure, lack of technical skills, smuggling and dumping, lack of access to credit, etc.), further trade liberalization, and strengthening the legal and judicial systems. The GoY may also be encouraged to pursue the policy of developing enclaves (industrial zones in

Hodeidah-Lahj-Abyan as well as Aden free zone) in which most of these bottlenecks are removed.

Services remained by far the largest contributor to GDP; constituting 48% of GDP in the 1990s. Despite its dominance in total output, the growth rate of the services value-added lagged behind agriculture and industrial sector recording an average growth rate of 5.0% during 1990-2000 and its contribution to GDP growth was less commensurate to its relative size in GDP. The services sector is dominated by government services (45% of services value-added in the 1990s) followed by transportation and communications, wholesale and retail trade, and real estate sectors. Services value-added is projected to increase by 8% per annum and to raise its contribution in GDP from 39% in 2000 to 43% by 2005. The plan puts heavy emphasis on tourism, transport and communications, and financial services with 11%, 9% and 12% annual growth rate targets, respectively.

Tourism has been identified by the SFYP as one of the most promising sectors to accelerate GDP growth and to increase rates of job creation. Yemen has huge potentials in tourism (e.g., historical, religious and archeological sites, coasts, islands, mountains and deserts). Including indirect related activities, tourism is estimated to have generated US$ 135 million and contributed slightly less than 2% of GDP in 2000. While the SFYP strives to increase tourism value-added by 11% per annum, this Report postulates that attainment of this target may be difficult in the current circumstances and projects increases in international business traffic by slightly more than the GDP growth rate and international vacation tourism to increase by up to three folds if the constraints affecting the sector are removed (e.g., security concerns, poor infrastructure, low capacity in certain destinations, cultural and religious barriers). Domestic tourism is likely to pick up commensurately with GDP growth.

The potentials for growth in the transport and communications sector are large and the current condition of the networks and the high cost of services represent major hindrances to economic activities and initiatives. Despite liberalization and deregulation efforts, the whole sector remained largely under control of state monopolies and the government also controls most of the tariffs and fares. Transport and communications services represent one-fifth of services value-added. Their share in GDP growth, however, continued to decline from about 15% in 1990 to 10% in 2000, and their contribution to GDP growth has been negative. The sub-sector recorded negative growth rates during 1993-1996 and only recovered in 1997-2000. The sector's value-added is projected to increase by 9.1% per annum over the SFYP in addition to specific targets for roads, telephones, air and freight traffic. This Report postulates that properly executed infrastructure investment (including by the Government) should be an important source of growth in Yemen and in particular the transport sector should be accorded a higher priority for its impact on other sectors. The main suggested policy reforms in the sector include: (i) sustained liberalization and deregulation, especially communications and air and land transport; (ii) promotion of private provision of services; (iii) creation of regulatory agencies independent from service provision, and; (v) liberalization of tariffs and fares.

Chapter 5 of the Report provides detailed analysis on potentials of each sector, major constraints, SFYP targets and their feasibility and proposes a set of policy actions and critical reforms to tap the potentials in these sectors. However, from the analysis, a number of constraints and obstacles cut across a number of sectors and those would require priority actions by the Government, specifically:

Improving governance and Sustained pursuit of policy reforms: Evidence suggests that weak governance remain the main obstacle for rapid economic growth in Yemen and the GoY has to embark on a bold program to improve governance structures in the country. In addition, the perusal of structural reforms is a key requisite to achieve in the SFYP' GDP growth targets, particularly given the low productivity growth which characterizes most of the economic sectors. This would require macroeconomic stability and marked improvements in the quality of human resources, further liberalization, deregulations and privatization, and marked improvements in the legal and judicial systems.

Enhancing domestic security: lack of security hampers activity in almost all economic sectors and in particular the envisaged growth targets of the promising sectors such as tourism, mining and extractive industries as well as investment targets (FDI and private domestic investments) are unlikely to be met without concerted efforts by the government to enhance domestic security.

Removing excessive and arbitrary regulations that resulted in weak infrastructures: Weak infrastructure and the implied high production costs seriously hamper private sector development, activity of most economic sectors and the competitiveness of Yemeni exports. Both public and private sectors should have complementary and important roles in increasing investments into the sector as well as in the provision of infrastructure itself.

Reforms of the legal and judicial systems: Weak legal and judicial systems coupled with weak enforcement of rulings, lack of clarifications of property rights, conflicts over land ownership are impeding developments and investments in almost all sectors of the economy. A comprehensive program for Judicial and Legal Reforms with special focus on commercial and business sector and land registration is critical for investment and economic growth.

Reforms of public administration: Efficiency in the delivery of public services is low due to weakness in public administration and inflated civil services. The GoY should seek to improve upon the delivery of government services by completion of the Civil Service Modernization Project and more efficient allocation of resources with more focus on the social sectors and maintenance and operations.

PART I:

ECONOMIC GROWTH:
PERFORMANCE AND STRUCTURE

CHAPTER 1:
ECONOMIC GROWTH AND MACROECONOMIC PERFORMANCE

INTRODUCTION AND CONTEXT

For the preparation of the Poverty Reduction Strategy Paper (PRSP), the Government of Yemen (GoY) requested the Bank for assistance in undertaking an in-depth examination of poverty and sources of, and constraints to, economic growth. Thus, this Report is prepared specifically to provide an analysis to the sources of economic growth in Yemen with special emphasis on potential economic sectors as well as the private sector environment and governance issues. The main objective of the study is to identify major constraints to faster economic growth and to draw forward-looking agenda and policy reforms measures to remove constraints in these sectors. High and sustained rates of economic growth in Yemen, as recognized by the PRSP, are necessary for the reduction of the high levels of unemployment and poverty in the country.

The first part of the Report reviews economic performance in Yemen and assesses the government medium- and long-term development plans. It provides a detailed analysis of the major structural characteristics of the Yemeni economy and the main economic sectors with the aim of identifying their constraints and potentials. This chapter reviews political and economic developments in Yemen before the unification to provide a historical context for the analysis of economic growth in the 1990s, highlights the trends in economic growth over the last decade with a demand and factor decomposition of growth and the contribution, as well as developments, of the economic sectors during the same period. It also assesses the impact of economic reforms undertaken in the mid-1990s on the trends and the structure of economic growth and reviews the medium-term economic plan and the long-term strategy vision for social and economic development. The Plan and the Strategy guide the GoY's future growth strategy and the PRSP is prepared within its framework. Chapter II analyzes in details the potentials and the constraints of the main economic sectors: agriculture, industry and services sectors. Three sub-sectors identified by the Second Five-Year Plan (SFYP) as "potential" and "promising" sectors for the attainment of growth targets are analyzed in depth (tourism, fisheries and manufacturing) as well as the oil sector given its large impact on other sectors and total GDP.

Part II of the Report is devoted to the study of Yemen' private sector environment and external competitiveness given the importance accorded to the private sector and exports in the medium- and long-term development plans. Private sector development is necessary for increasing capital accumulation and raising productivity, which are essential for long-term economic growth, and export-orientation is key to rapid income growth in small countries like Yemen. Chapter III attempts to investigate why private sector's response to stabilization and structural reforms in Yemen has been slow. It highlights the results of a survey that was undertaken specifically for this study for about 1,000 private enterprises in five governorates in Yemen in November 2001. This chapter also provides important elements for future reform agenda for developing the private sector and improving governance in Yemen. Chapter IV focuses on external trade and export performance in the 1990s with special emphasis on external competitiveness, which underpins export growth.

Given the policy relevance of the analytical work undertaken for this study, Part III of the Report concludes with policy recommendations including a concise policy matrix for accelerating and sustaining economic growth in Yemen in the medium- and long-terms. The recommended reforms take into consideration the existing potentials and constraints of the main economic sectors, the objectives of the medium- and long-term development plans and the feasibility and sequencing of the policy reforms. This part of the Report is, therefore, intended to provide an input into the PRSP and into deliberations among the Bank, the GoY and stakeholders on future economic reforms in Yemen.

The review of the trends in economic growth in Yemen in the 1990s suggests that economic growth has been very volatile and the volatility has been driven mainly by exogenous factors. Major policy changes and debt reduction have made only a partial and small impact on economic growth. Services sector remained the largest contributor to total output and economic growth. The share of industrial valued-added in total output is remarkably small in comparison with similar countries though it has been dynamic in the 1990s and contributed to GDP growth more than its commensurate size in total output. Decomposition of Yemen's GDP to demand components in the 1990s reveals that domestic demand (and consumption in particular) contributed to most of the GDP growth in the early 1990s. External demand made a significant contribution to GDP growth after the implementation of trade and macroeconomic reforms in mid-1990s. In particular, most of the GDP growth is attributed to external demand in 1996, 1999 and 2000. Finally, GDP growth was primarily driven by factor accumulation (labor and capital) while TFP was negative for most of the 1990s pointing to substantial scope for structural reforms to improve non-oil output without necessarily higher levels of investment.

The GoY sets ambitious targets for GDP growth in the medium- and long-terms. These targets are, however, far from the actual performance of total GDP and sector growth rates in the 1990s and unless deeper structural reforms at the macro-level and at sectoral levels, the challenge of meeting these growth targets will be difficult to achieve. The GoY is also counting on generating economic growth by increasing domestic demand in anticipation of weaker external demand (due to expected decline in oil production). This may set a limit to targeted growth potentials and more efforts to enhance non-oil exports are necessary for realization of high and sustained GDP growth in Yemen. Furthermore, the SFYP emphasis on public investment relative to private investment is quite high and may undermine macroeconomic stability and efficiency of investment in Yemen.

POLITICAL AND ECONOMIC DEVELOPMENTS BEFORE UNIFICATION

The Republic of Yemen (RoY) emerged in 1990, following the unification of the Yemen Arab Republic (YAR) and the People's Democratic Republic of Yemen (PDRY). Unification was a long-standing aspiration of Yemeni citizens, though both countries wanted to achieve it under their own political and ideological agenda. Relations between the two republics were dominated by suspicions, political tension, and strains that resulted in several border clashes and two wars. In May 1990, following major political and economic developments at the domestic and international levels,[1] unification became a reality and a new era of dramatic social and economic development started.

The two former republics followed completely different paths for their political and economic development and as a result achieved somewhat diverse outcomes and most of the current economic, social and political problems are partly attributed to those differences. North Yemen was ruled for decades by a feudal royalist system after the defeat of the Ottomans in 1919. The medieval rule of

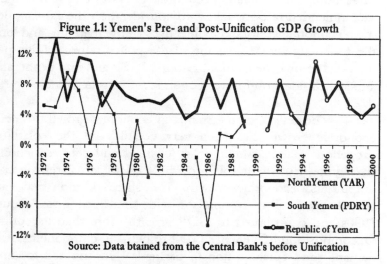

Figure 1.1: Yemen's Pre- and Post-Unification GDP Growth

Source: Data btained from the Central Bank's before Unification

the Imam resulted in backward economic structure, primitive infrastructure and weak human resources because of isolationist policies and the absence of formal education. An army revolution overthrew the last Imam in 1962 and formed the YAR. Soon after, the new regime was trapped in a civil war with the royalists, which lasted for eight years. Since 1970, YAR adopted a market-based economic system though the government had played an important role in the economy through establishment of public enterprises and excessive regulations. External trade and private investment were allowed but were heavily regulated by protective trade policies. YAR achieved some progress in economic development and less so in the social sector. Workers' remittances[2] and foreign assistance —as well as oil exports starting in 1987— were the main sources of foreign exchanges.

South Yemen was colonized by Britain for about a century and a half when the British took Aden by force from the Ottomans in 1839. The colonial rule was mostly concentrated in Aden, which gained prominence as a strategic transit port as well as a commercial center after the opening of the Suez Canal. Other provinces in the South were practically ruled by traditional feudal systems under the protection of the British ruler. During colonial rule, economic development took place only in Aden while the rest of the country was kept underdeveloped. The territory gained independence in 1967 when the nationalist forces took over the whole country, including the protectorates ruled by the monarchial systems, and consequently declared the formation of the PDRY. In contrast with YAR, the PDRY's government inherited a well-developed Capital city with basic infrastructure, relatively well-organized public administration and well-developed human resources.

---

[1]   These developments included, among others, the decline in foreign assistance (e.g., the collapse of the Soviet Union), discovery of oil in both countries, and the various economic difficulties encountered by both republics by the end of the 1980s.

[2]   A large part of the labor force (as high as 30% in YAR) were workers abroad, see World Bank (2001; 1).

After independence, PDRY adopted the socialist command-and-control system. Every aspect of economic activity was totally controlled and managed by the government, which additionally confiscated and nationalized private enterprises that were established during the British rule. The government also redistributed half of the country's cultivated land among landless families and began investments in education and other social services. The policies pursued in PDRY, however, resulted in poor economic outcomes despite relative success in human resources development (health and education). Reforms of agriculture, fisheries and ports all failed to realize their objectives. Workers' remittances, which constituted about half of government revenues, declined in the late 1980s and, with the precipitous decline in the financial assistance from the Soviet Union, foreign debt reached 180% of GDP by the late 1980s.

Trends in Economic Growth in the Former Republics

The pre-unification trends in economic growth in the former republics are difficult to depict because of lack of detailed data, particularly in the former PDRY.[3] Both countries experienced major fluctuations in GDP growth during 1970-1990 due to their dependence on workers' remittances and foreign aid. They enjoyed relatively high growth in the 1970s due to the oil boom in the Gulf States (Figure 1.1). By the mid-1970s both countries were growing at 7-9% per annum. Following the decline in oil prices in the 1980s, both countries witnessed slowdown in economic growth as a result of drop-off in workers' remittances. Economic growth also declined because of the reduction in foreign aid, though each country used to receive foreign assistance from a different source.[4] Although economic growth in YAR in the 1980s was lower than in the previous decade, the country managed to maintain positive and small GDP growth rates throughout the 1980s and the severity of the volatility of growth was less in comparison with the PDRY.

Macroeconomic disequilibria characterized both economies in the 1980s, mainly due to increasing fiscal deficits. In the PDRY, government spending as a ratio of GDP increased from an average of 49% in the 1970s to 77% in the 1980s without corresponding increases in government revenues and consequently average fiscal deficit increased from 20% of GDP to 36% over the same period. Similarly, government spending in YAR increased from 16% of GDP in the 1970s to 35% in the 1980s and the fiscal deficit increased from 3% of GDP to 13% over the same period. Most of the deficit in both countries was financed by the central banks, which kept inflation in double digits. External debt also increased in both countries to unsustainable levels. Furthermore, both countries had by the late 1980s, large civil service, loss-making public enterprisers, restrictive trade regimes and overvalued exchange rates.

---

[3]   As in many other socialist centrally-planned economies, national accounts in the PDRY focused mainly on gross national income and net material product. GDP at current market prices was computed but there was no GDP deflator. The IMF and World Bank, however, had some estimates for real GDP growth for some years during 1970-1989.

[4]   YAR obtained most of its foreign aid from Saudi Arabia and Kuwait while PDRY got most of its economic and military aid from the former Soviet Union.

ECONOMIC GROWTH IN THE 1990S

Based on the newly revised national accounts in the RoY (see Annex A on national accounts data), GDP growth averaged 4.1% during 1991-1994, picked up to 8.3% during 1995-1997, and decelerated to 4.6% during 1998-2000. For the whole decade, GDP increased by an annual average of 5.5%. This growth performance compares favorably with average growth rates for low-income countries and the countries in the MENA region (Figure 1.2),

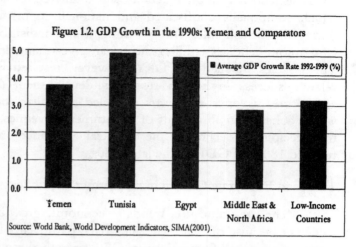

Figure 1.2: GDP Growth in the 1990s: Yemen and Comparators

■ Average GDP Growth Rate 1992-1999 (%)

Yemen, Tunisia, Egypt, Middle East & North Africa, Low-Income Countries

Source: World Bank, World Development Indicators, SIMA(2001).

although it lagged behind Egypt and Tunisia, the two best performers in the region. Moreover, despite the good overall GDP growth, with the population growth rates of almost 4.0% during 1990-2000, GDP per capita increased by only 1.5% over the same period (box 1.1).

BOX 1.1: PER CAPITA GDP GROWTH

High population growth rate in Yemen meant that real growth in GDP per capita is quite small in comparison with total GDP growth rate. GDP growth rate in Yemen has remained positive throughout 1991-2001, but GDP per capita actually declined in 1991 (due also to return of about million Yemenis from the Gulf), 1994 and 2001. GNP per capita declined in 1991, 1993, 1994, 1999 and 2001.

	1991	1992	1993	1994	1995	1996	1997	1998	1999	2000	2001*
GDP, real growth rate (%)	2.0	8.3	4.1	2.2	10.9	5.9	8.1	4.9	3.6	5.1	1.8
GDP per capita, real growth rate (%)	-9.7	4.9	0.7	-1.1	7.5	2.9	5.1	2.0	0.9	2.4	-1.0
GNP per capita, real growth rate (%)	-13.4	5.9	-0.4	-7.2	8.4	5.5	7.8	8.7	-2.8	2.8	-0.5
GNP per capita, Atlas Method US$	..	390	370	290	270	280	330	380	390	420	460

Source: Data from the World Bank, Live Database: * Estimates.

Actual per capita growth rates could be lower than the above estimates if the GoY' population growth rates were used. Therefore, growth performance of Yemen relative to comparators looks worse if undertaken on the basis of per capita incomes (see Annex B for discussion on differences in the estimates of population growth rates).

The Early 1990s: Pre-Reforms Period and Macro-Shocks

Growth pattern in Yemen was not universal throughout the 1990s. The period 1990-1994 witnessed several major shocks and as a result major fluctuations in annual GDP growth rates. First, a severe drought affected agricultural activity in 1990 and 1991. Second, a precipitous drop in workers' remittances and external aid followed the Gulf war in 1991 and about one million Yemenis returned from the Gulf States. Nonetheless, GDP growth recovered strongly by more than 8% in 1992. Third, and following the high initial costs of unification, political instability culminated into a civil war in 1994 with massive destruction to lives and property. Consequently, output growth decelerated to 2.2% in 1994 and inflation increased markedly. The current account deficit averaged 18.5% of GDP during 1991-1993, and by 1994, fiscal deficit was 15% of GDP, inflation rate was 71%, and external debt mounted. After initial price liberalization efforts in early 1990-1991, the GoY addressed the financial imbalances through direct controls of the economy restricting imports and investment and movements of the exchange and interest rates. In 1994, some steps were taken by the authorities to achieve positive real interest rates and more realistic exchange rates (Table 1.1).

TABLE 1.1: MACROECONOMIC INDICATORS IN YEMEN, 1991-2000

Year	GDP Growth, (%)	Non-Oil GDP, (%)	Oil Value-Added, (%)	Inflation, CPI, (%)	Fiscal Balance (% of GDP)
1991	2.0	3.2	-5.6	44.9	-3.5
1992	8.3	11.7	-15.4	50.6	-11.9
1993	4.1	4.0	4.2	54.8	-12.8
1994	2.2	-2.3	42.7	71.3	-14.7
1995	10.9	9.4	19.9	62.5	-5.2
1996	5.9	4.5	13.5	40.0	-0.9
1997	8.1	8.2	7.5	4.6	-1.5
1998	4.9	5.4	2.5	11.5	-7.9
1999	3.7	2.9	7.8	8.0	0.1
2000	5.1	4.7	7.2	8.5	7.9

Source: Data from the World Bank, Live Database (2001).

Economic Growth During the Period of Reforms, 1995-2000

The macroeconomic policy mix and outcomes differed radically between the first and the second halves of the 1990s. With the achievement of political stability in mid-1990s, GoY started on an ambitious program for economic reforms and stabilization in early 1995. The program aimed to enhance the foundations of a market-based and private sector led economy. It focused on stabilization, price and trade liberalization, fiscal adjustments and reform of the exchange rate regime. Interest rates were liberalized and monetary policy was tightened. The Yemeni Rial (YR) was devalued substantially, a market exchange regime was introduced and a floating rate regime was adopted in 1996. A number of structural reforms were also implemented. Tariffs were reduced and their structure was simplified. Investment regulations were also streamlined and a privatization program for public enterprises and banks initiated. Stricter prudential regulations for banks were introduced. Furthermore, the period 1995-1997 witnessed significant reduction in external debt. Following the rescheduling of Paris Club in 1996, external debt was reduced from 173% of GDP in 1996 to 80% by end-1999 and debt services declined from about 32% of exports earnings to 11%.[5]

Inflation rates continued to decline and reached a single digit in 1997 reflecting success in reducing the fiscal deficit (averaging 2.5% of GDP), which allowed for tight monetary growth (Figure 1.3).[6] As a response to the stabilization and reforms measures and assisted by higher growth in oil value-added (averaging 14%), GDP growth recovered to an average of 8.3% during 1995-1997 and non-oil GDP picked up by 7.1% during the same period (see Figure 1.4). GDP growth then decelerated to 4.6% during 1998-2000 because of the collapse of oil prices in 1998 and the deceleration in the non-oil GDP growth in 1999. High oil prices in 2000 improved macroeconomic indicators and stabilization indicators continued to improve. In 2000, fiscal and current account balances maintained record surplus and inflation remained low at 10%.

---

[5]   See also World Bank (2001) and IMF (2001; 28).

[6]   Inflation declined slowly at the beginning of the program because of adjustments in administered prices.

13

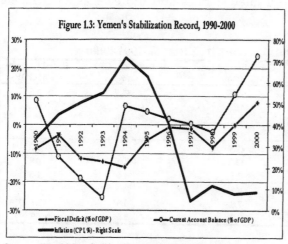

Figure 1.3: Yemen's Stabilization Record, 1990-2000

Source: World Bank. Live Database (LDB), 2001.

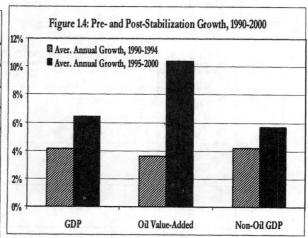

Figure 1.4: Pre- and Post-Stabilization Growth, 1990-2000

Source: World Bank. Live Database (LDB), 2001.

Sectoral Contribution to GDP and Economic Growth, 1990-2000

There has not been much change in the relative importance of economic sectors in total output in the 1990s. Services remained by far the largest contributor to GDP; constituting 48% of GDP during 1990-2000. This relative importance of services to total GDP is relatively higher than the corresponding ratio in the group of low-income countries (42%) and the average for the MENA region (46%). It compares with the ratio of middle-income countries (51%) over the same period.[7] Despite its dominance in total output, the growth rate of the services value-added lagged behind agriculture and industrial sector recording an average growth rate of 5.0% during 1991-2000 and its contribution to GDP growth was less than its relative size in total GDP (Table 1.2).

TABLE 1.2: SECTORAL CONTRIBUTION TO GDP IN YEMEN, 1991-2000

Sector		1991-1994	1995-2000	1991-2000
Total GDP	Growth Rate (%)	4.8	6.4	5.9
Agriculture	Growth Rate (%)	6.3	5.8	5.9
	Share in GDP (%)	22.1	17.8	19.0
	Contribution to GDP Growth (%)	1.4	1.0	1.1
	Share in GDP Growth (%)	28.9	16.0	19.3
Industry	Growth Rate (%)	4.4	8.8	7.3
	Share in GDP (%)	23.3	37.6	33.3
	Contribution to GDP Growth (%)	1.0	3.3	2.4
	Share in GDP Growth (%)	21.0	51.9	41.4
Services	Growth Rate (%)	4.4	5.4	5.0
	Share in GDP (%)	54.7	44.6	47.7
	Contribution to GDP Growth (%)	2.4	2.4	2.4
	Share in GDP Growth (%)	50.1	37.3	41.0

Source: Computed by staff based on data from the World Bank, Live Database (LDB); 2001.

The most striking feature of Yemen's output structure has been the relatively small contribution of the industrial sector to GDP. Despite being an oil exporting country throughout the 1990s, the share of the industrial sector in Yemen (32.7% of GDP) lagged

---

[7] The large size of the rent economy (oil, workers remittances, etc.) is argued to have been a cause behind the large size of the services sector.

behind the averages for low-income countries, Sub-Saharan Africa and the MENA region.[8] In particular, the share of manufacturing in total GDP in Yemen (9%) is about half of the sector's contribution in Sub-Saharan Africa. The rate of growth of manufacturing value-added in the 1990s, however, was higher in Yemen than in Sub-Saharan Africa and low-income countries (Table 1.3).

TABLE 1.3: CONTRIBUTION OF INDUSTRY TO GDP, YEMEN AND COMPARATORS, 1990-1999

	Industry (% of GDP)	Industry, Average Growth Rate	Manuf. (% of GDP)	Manuf., Average Growth Rate	Non-Manuf. Industrial Output (% of GDP)	Non-Manuf. Industry, Average Growth Rate
Yemen	**26.8**	**6.5**	**9.0**	**4.0**	**17.8**	**8.5**
Low- Income	29.9	2.4	18.5	2.3	11.5	2.6
Middle- Income	36.1	4.1	24.5	6.0	11.6	0.8
Middle East & North Africa	40.9	2.6 *	12.9	3.4 *	28.0	2.3 *
Lower Middle-Income	37.6	5.3	27.5	8.6	10.1	-1.5
Sub-Saharan África	29.7	1.2	15.7	1.1	14.0	1.3
Low- & Middle-Income	35.1	3.8	23.5	5.4	11.6	1.1

* = Average for 1991-1997 only; and Manuf. stands for manufacturing.
Source: computed from data derived from the World Bank, World Development Indicators, SIMA (2001).

Industrial activity grew by 4.4% during 1991-1994, picked up in the post-civil war recording an average growth rate of 15% during 1995-1997, and decelerated to 5.5% during 1998-2000. For the whole decade, the industrial sector grew by an average rate of 7.3% and was very dynamic because its contribution to GDP growth was more than commensurate to its relative share in GDP especially in the late 1990s. Half of the industrial output in Yemen in the 1990s was constituted by oil and mining.

The share of agriculture value-added in Yemen's GDP averaged 19.5% during 1990-2000. This was slightly lower than the corresponding share of low-income countries in the 1990s (27%) but is much higher than the average for the MENA water-constrained region (13.5%). Although its contribution to GDP is relatively small, agriculture provides 58% of total employment and livelihood and income for about 77% of total population. The sector's contribution to GDP growth in the 1990s was in line with its relative share in total GDP.

DEMAND AND FACTOR DECOMPOSITION OF GDP GROWTH

Decomposition of Yemen's GDP to demand components in the 1990s reveals that domestic demand (and consumption in particular) contributed to most of the GDP growth during 1991-1993. External demand contributed negatively to GDP growth during these years. External demand made a significant contribution to GDP growth after the implementation of trade and macroeconomic reforms in mid-1990s. In particular, most of the GDP growth is attributed to external demand in 1996, 1999 and 2000. The SFYP projects weaker external demand (due to expected decline in oil production) and strives to achieve the growth targets by solely depending on domestic demand (consumption and investment). This may set a limit to future growth prospects and efforts to enhance non-oil exports will be critical for the realization of high and sustained GDP growth. It seems also that the GoY is counting on a significantly reduced rate of import growth that may be inconsistent with high GDP growth targets in the medium-term (Table 1.4).

---

[8] The share of the industrial sector was very high in 1999 and 2000, pushing the average share for the whole decade, the share during 1990-1998 was only 30%.

TABLE 1.4: DEMAND DECOMPOSITION OF GDP GROWTH (%)

	1991	1992	1993	1994	1995	1996	1997	1998	1999	2000	2001	2002	2003	2004	2005
	Actual										SFYP Targets				
Net Exports	-16.5	-2.1	-7.7	8.9	-3.3	18.2	-0.5	-13.4	8.4	15.8	-2.0	-1.7	-2.0	-2.0	-2.1
Exports	-0.3	-0.7	2.5	0.6	10.0	19.0	0.1	-6.9	10.0	16.8	-1.5	-0.9	-0.9	-1.2	-1.1
Imports	16.2	1.4	10.1	-8.3	13.3	0.8	0.6	6.6	1.6	0.9	0.5	0.8	1.2	0.8	1.0
Consumption	19.7	5.6	13.7	-5.1	11.9	-16.3	3.8	16.8	-2.8	-13.0	3.6	4.1	4.4	4.1	4.5
Investment	-1.3	4.9	-1.9	-1.7	2.2	4.0	4.8	1.6	-1.9	2.3	2.8	3.1	3.3	3.4	3.7
Real GDP Growth	2.0	8.3	4.1	2.2	10.9	5.9	8.1	4.9	3.7	5.1	4.4	5.5	5.7	5.6	6.1

Source: Staff estimates based on data from the Central Statistical Organization (CSO) and the Second Five Year Plan (SFYP).

Factor Decomposition of GDP and TFP

Total factor productivity estimates for Yemen are derived assuming a standard new-classical Cobb-Douglas Production function.[9] While poor data and short time-series prevent making strong conclusions from the analysis, it is clear that GDP growth was primarily driven by factor accumulation (labor and capital) while TFP was negative for most of the 1990s pointing to substantial scope for structural reforms to improve non-oil output without necessarily higher levels of investment (Table 1.5).

The growth accounting exercise (Table 1.5) shows that TFP was substantially negative in the pre-reform period even under different assumptions on initial stock of capital and capital-output share. Productivity improved with the introduction of policy reforms as can be seen on TFP growth estimates for the period 1995-1997. These results are consistent with previous estimates of TFP in Yemen and with the prevailing trends in TFP growth in the MENA region.[10]

TABLE 1.5: TOTAL FACTOR PRODUCTIVITY (TFP) ESTIMATES

Year	Growth Rates (%)			TFP Estimates (%)					
	GDP	Employment	Investment	$K_0 =$ GDP/2 $\alpha = 0.4$	$K_0 =$ GDP/2 $\alpha = 0.7$	$K_0=$GDP $\alpha = 0.4$	$K_0=$GDP $\alpha = 0.7$	$K_0=$ 1.5*GDP $\alpha = 0.4$	$K_0=$ 1.5*GDP $\alpha = 0.7$
1991	2.0	3.3	14.4	-8.9	-5.2	-3.9	-2.7	-2.0	-1.7
1992	8.3	3.4	4.3	-5.1	-0.1	0.5	2.7	2.8	3.9
1993	4.1	3.4	4.3	-5.4	-2.4	-1.9	-0.6	-0.2	0.2
1994	2.2	3.4	4.6	-5.5	-3.4	-2.9	-2.1	-1.6	-1.4
1995	10.9	3.2	4.1	2.4	5.0	5.0	6.3	6.4	7.0
1996	5.9	2.9	2.9	-3.8	-0.4	-1.1	1.0	0.5	1.8
1997	8.1	5.0	2.9	-3.2	0.0	-0.6	1.2	1.0	2.0
1998	4.9	3.7	2.8	-6.4	-2.6	-4.0	-1.4	-2.5	-0.6
1999	3.7	2.9	2.7	-4.5	-1.8	-3.0	-1.1	-1.9	-0.5
2000	5.1	3.6	2.4	-3.5	-1.0	-2.1	-0.3	-1.1	0.2
1990-2000	5.5	3.5	3.5	-4.4	-1.2	-1.4	0.3	0.1	1.1

Source: Staff estimates.

---

[9]   The estimated Cobb-Douglas production function: $Y = A \, L^\alpha \, K^{(1-\alpha)}$, where Y = total output, L = employment, K = capital, α = labor/output production share, and A = total factor productivity. Employment data are obtained from Ministry of Planning and Development for 1994-2000, estimates for 1990-1993 were extrapolated using CSO estimates for 1988. Capital stock is estimated as $K_t = (1-\delta) * K_{t-1} + FCA_t$, where δ is depreciation and assumed at 3%, FCA is fixed capital formation. K_0 (for 1989) was assumed to be equal to 0.5*GDP, GDP, and 1.5*GDP, respectively. Given the short-time series for Yemen, α was not estimated but assumed to be in the range of 0.7 and 0.4. GDP figures and FCA are from the World Bank LDB.

[10]   Similar results and conclusions were reached by the IMF (2001) study, which showed negative TFP for the whole 1990s, and improvements in the post-reform period. See also Dasgupta et al. (2001) for TFP growth trends in the MENA region and the impact of structural reforms on TFP.

Total investment as ratio of GDP fluctuated considerably during the FFYP. It increased from 22.1% in 1995 until it peaked in 1998 at 32.6% and then continued to decline reaching only 19.2% in 2000. Private investment, which peaked at 20% in 1997, continued to decline in the subsequent three years reaching only 10% by the end of the FFYP (Table 1.6). The SFYP, nonetheless, puts more emphasis on public investment. For the period 2001-2005, the government's planned ratio of public to private investments is extra-ordinary high and ranges from 61% (in the last year) to 81% (in the first years). In 1998, 95% of countries in the world had ratios less than 38% and 99% had ratios less than 77%.[11] Given the current levels of efficiency in public spending in Yemen and weak governance (chapter 3),[12] this emphasis on public spending is likely to undermine macroeconomic stability and efficiency of total investments in the country.

TABLE 1.6: TRENDS IN PRIVATE AND PUBLIC INVESTMENT, 1990-2005

| | Actual Figures | | | | | | | | | | | SFYP Targets | | | | |
	1990	1991	1992	1993	1994	1995	1996	1997	1998	1999	2000	2001	2002	2003	2004	2005
GDI (% of GDP)	15	16	22	20	21	22	23	25	33	25	19	21	23	24	26	29
Total fixed investment (% of GDP)	12	14	20	18	19	21	22	22	32	23	18	20	21	23	25	27
Private GDI (% of GDP)	6	13	20	17	19	19	16	20	16	14	10	11	13	14	16	18
Public GDI (% of GDP)	8	4	3	3	2	4	8	5	17	10	9	9	10	10	11	11
ICOR		7	1.6	4.1	6.5	1.1	2.2	2.0	3.9	5.4	3.4	6.3	5.6	4.8	4.6	4.4
Ratio of Private investment to GDI (%)	43	77	87	85	90	84	67	80	49	58	53	55	57	58	60	62

Source: Data for 1990-1999 are from the World Bank Live Database (LDB) and for 2000-2005 are from the Second Five-Year Plan (SFYP). The two series may not be compatible.[13]

Growth Targets of the 2025 Vision and the Second Five-Year Plan (SFYP)

Regardless of the different systems adopted, the two former republics undertook development planning with a focus on building basic physical, social and institutional infrastructures. A Three-Year Plan (1971-1973) was adopted in the PYDR and a Three-Year Development Program (1973-1975) was implemented in the YAR. These plans were followed by five-year plans until the unification in 1990. Following this tradition, the RoY implemented the First Five-Year Plan (FFYP) during 1996-2000. Average annual GDP growth during the FFYP was 5.5% (the Plan's target was 7.2%) and translated into a 2.0% increase in GDP *per capita*. Non-oil GDP recorded a lower growth rate of 5.1%. The low performing sectors included transportation and storage and manufacturing. On the other hand, fisheries and construction sub-sectors outperformed all other sectors and grew by more than 12% during 1996-2000.

The inability to meet the targets of the FFYP were attributed by the GoY to: (i) stabilization measures of the Economic, Financial and Administrative Reform program (EFARP) which coincided with the plan, and (ii) weak performance of specific sectors (particularly, transportation and communications, manufacturing and oil refining and to some extent the agricultural sector) despite better than expected performance of other sectors such as oil, fisheries, public utilities and construction activities. However, it should be pointed that fiscal policy was not deflationary under the FFYP. The weakening of growth

---

[11]   See World Bank, World Development Indicators (WDI).

[12]   See also World Bank (2001 b).

[13]   The SFYP had two inconsistent estimates for private sector investment.

performance could be attributed also to the deterioration in the expenditure structure (with much public employment and subsidies and little public investment), deteriorating governance and slow structural change.

Long- and Medium-Term Targets for Economic Growth in Yemen

During the implementation of the FFYP, the authorities decided to prepare the Second Five-Year Plan (SFYP) within a long-term strategy. Thus, the Strategic Vision 2025 was formulated to serve three objectives: (a) development of long-term solutions to deal with challenges that require longer interventions and continuous revisions through medium-term plans; (b) mobilization of all social and economic resources to address difficulties and constraints; and, (c) combination of traditional and innovative interventions based on social and economic realities. The Vision Strategy aims to upgrade human resources and to improve the living standards through improvement in health services, eradication of illiteracy, increase in enrollment ratios for basic education, and raising income *per capita* to the levels of middle-income countries through diversification of the economy, export promotion and job creation.

Under the Vision 2025, real GDP per capita is planned to increase by an annual average of 9% in the coming 25 years and population growth to slow gradually. Foreign and domestic investments are projected to increase significantly to meet the growth targets in addition to productivity increase in non-oil sectors. The sources of growth and potential sectors for the realization of growth targets stated in the Vision Strategy include the following: (a) promotion of tourism, especially in coastal areas; (b) enhancement of manufacturing based on Yemen's competitive advantages and development of small- and medium-scale industries; (c) development of extractive industries (mainly oil, gas and minerals) and reliance on natural gas as a main source of energy; (d) development of the agricultural sector by raising irrigation efficiency, encouragement of off-farm activities, and reduction of Qat plantations; (e) sustainable utilization of fish resources; (f) promotion of exports and increased integration in the world economy by utilization of FTAs and attraction of FDI; and (g) exploitation of the strategic location of Yemen and promotion of Free Zones.

Four necessary conditions were singled out in the Vision Strategy for the attainment of the GDP growth targets: (a) effective partnership between private and public sectors and reliance on the private sector as the main engine of growth; (b) creation of a conducive environment for private sector development through civil service modernization, restructuring of the roles of government agencies, simplification of regulations, decentralization, and reform of the legal and judicial systems; (c) poverty reduction by halving food poverty in 2015 and its complete eradication by 2025, reduction of upper poverty levels to 10% in 2025, expansion of the social safety net, job creation through micro-enterprises and community-driven development; and, (d) environmental protection through efficient management of natural resources, prevention of pollution of water basins, management of solid waste, and coastal protection.

The SFYP was prepared to be the first medium-term development plan within the framework of the Vision 2025 Strategy. Its main axes include the development of human resources, achieving economic stability and diversification, private sector development, export promotion, good governance and decentralization, and environmental sustainability. The targets of the plan include: (i) achieving real GDP growth of 5.6% per annum (8% for non-oil GDP); (ii) attracting private and foreign investment to raise total private investment to 58% of total investments; (iii) increasing the contribution of commodity sectors (between 6.1% to 13%); (iv) reducing underemployment to 22%; (v) reducing poverty to 21.7% by the end of the plan; (vi) achieving a balanced budget; and (vii) curbing inflationary pressures to an average rate of 4.9%. The SFYP seeks to achieve an increase in total investment from 19.2% of GDP in 2000, to 28.6% by the end of the Plan. This increase depends on the achievement of a high nominal growth in private investment of about 24%, and 15% for public sector investment (18% increase for Government investments and 10% for oil investments). Consequently, the share of private sector investment in total investment is expected to increase from 53.2% in 2000 to 61.8% by 2005 (Table 1.7).

TABLE 1.7: TARGETS OF THE SECOND FIVE-YEAR PLAN (SFYP)
(Billions of Constant Yemeni Rials unless otherwise stated)

	2000	2005	Average Annual Growth Rate (%)
Total GDP	1,379	1,812	5.6
Non-Oil GDP	914	1,346	8.0
Oil GDP	465	465	0.0
Private Sector	605	973	9.1
Government Sector	308	373	3.9
Agriculture, Forestry & Fisheries, VA	195	263	6.1
O/w Fisheries	15	29	13.0
Services, VA	380	589	9.1
O/w Tourism	10	16	10.7
Manufacturing	67	108	10.0
Construction	58	98	11.0
Electricity, Water and Gas	9	14	9.2

Source: Derived from Table 2-5, page 140 of the Second Five-Year Plan (SFYP, 2001).

While the five-year Incremental Capital Output Ratio (ICOR) was 3.36 in 2000,[14] the SFYP investment and growth figure imply an average ICOR of 5.2.[15] Therefore, the investment levels envisaged under the plan may be very high to achieve the targeted GDP growth rate of 5.6%. Furthermore, in real terms these investment figures project increases in private investment by an annual average of 21% and public investment by 13% over the plan period.[16]

---

[14] The five-year average ICOR in Yemen in 2000 was only 3.14.

[15] This Report does not adopt the Harrod-Domar growth model. Easterly (1997) provided evidence on the lack of theoretical and empirical justification for assuming a short-run proportional relationship between investment and growth. Deverjan et. al. (2000) also provided evidence that public investment is not correlated with growth in Africa.

[16] In an attempt to calculate real growth rates projected for GDP and demand components (which were not available in the SFYP document), the constant prices series have been estimated based on the current prices data and using GDP deflator (for GDP and all demand components). It has been observed that the projected growth rates based on GDP deflator are different from the plan targets. It seems that instead the CPI inflation rates were used in the estimation. In both cases, real average growth rates for total investment under the plan are set at very high levels (between 14.3% to 15.5% depending on choice of deflator). Staff estimate from figures not published in the SFYP is that the GDP deflator used in projections is 4.8% in 2001, 5.8% in 2002, 6.6% in 2003, 7.3% in 2004, 7.7% in 2005 with an average of 6.4% over the plan and not 4%

Sectoral Composition and Growth Targets of the Second Five Year Plan (SFYP)

The SFYP does not envisage major structural changes in the sectoral composition of GDP. It, nonetheless, plans to raise the contribution of non-oil sectors into the GDP from 71% in 2000 to 75% by the end of the plan. This is expected to take place as a result of an 8.0% average annual targeted growth rate of non-oil sectors while real oil value-added is expected to stagnate over the plan period.

Although the Strategic Vision 2025 strives to increase GDP growth in the next 25 years by an average rate of 9.0%, the SFYP targets an average growth rate of 5.6% which appears reasonable by Yemen's historical growth standards (5.5% actual rate achieved over the FFYP and 4.5% during 1990-1995). The plan, nonetheless, puts ambitious targets for agricultural and services sectors, which exceeded historical growth patterns of both sectors throughout the 1990s (Chapter 2). As targeted under the FFYP, the agricultural sector is planned to increase its output by an annual average of 6.7% while it only managed to grow by 5.5% over the FFYP. Similarly, services value-added is planned to increase by 8.0% per annum over the SFYP while the sector managed to grow by an annual average of 5.3% during the FFYP. Finally, the SFYP predicts a moderate growth of the industrial sector (3.0% per annum), mainly due to expected stagnation in oil value-added. It should be stated that the industrial sector was the only sector that managed to meet, and exceed over, planned targets during the FFYP again due to better than expected contribution of the oil sector (Table 1.8).

TABLE 1.8: YEMEN GDP BY SECTOR, 1990-2005

	Share of GDP (%)				Average Annual Growth Rate (%)			
			End-FFYP	Target End-SFYP	Actual	Target FFYP	Actual FFYP	Target SFYP
	1990	1995	2000	2005	1990-1995	1996-2000	1996-2000	2001-2005
Agriculture, value-added	24.2	19.4	15.3	16.1	2.9	7.0	5.5	6.7
Industry, value-added	26.8	32.2	46.2	40.9	5.5	4.0	6.5	3.0
Services, value added	47.9	48.3	38.5	43.1	4.8	8.7	5.3	8.0
Non-Oil GDP	86.6	86.5	70.9	74.3	4.2	8.4	5.1	8.0
Total GDP	100.0	100.0	100.0	100.0	4.5	7.2	5.5	5.6

Sources: Central Statistical Organization (CSO) for 1990-2000, First Five-Year Plan (FFYP) for targets over 1996-2000, and the Second Five-Year (SFYP) for 2001-2005.

CHAPTER 2:
POTENTIALS AND CONSTRAINTS OF THE MAIN ECONOMIC SECTORS

INTRODUCTION AND MAJOR FINDINGS

This chapter reviews the main economic sectors in Yemen, their contribution to GDP growth and their existing potentials and constraints. It also assesses the sectoral targets set in the SFYP and the Vision 2025 Strategy in the light of the observed constraints and potentials. The review gives special emphasis to the "potential sectors" identified by the GoY in the SFYP and the Strategy Vision 2025 (tourism, manufacturing, fisheries, and oil and gas). The assessment reveals that Yemen has good potentials in most economic sectors (particularly gas, mining, tourism and manufacturing), although it will face shortages in oil, water and fish resources if no additional resources are discovered or existing resources are not managed in a sustainable way. This calls for efficient utilization of existing resources and addressing cross-sectoral constraints (e.g., insecurity, excessive regulation, difficult access to land, under-pricing of water and diesel, *etc.*) as well as removal of constraints in specific sectors.

Yemen has huge potentials in the agricultural sector and achieving an average growth rate of 6.7% per annum during the SFYP appears to be an ambitious, though achievable, target for the sector. Excluding fisheries, agricultural output is planned to increase by 6.1% per annum and realizing this target is confronted with severe water shortages, vulnerability to fluctuations in rainfall, rapid deforestation and desertification, prevalence of traditional cultivation techniques and rapid expansion in Qat plantation. Nonetheless, given the substantial yield gap, huge post-harvest losses, value-added of most crops can grow faster than the plan's target if productivity is increased, cultivated area is expanded and Qat plantations are controlled. Raising fisheries output by 13% annually also appears to be a reasonable target because the sector managed to grow by even faster rates in the last couple of years. However, the projected utilization of fish resources could represent over-exploitation and risk the collapse of the fish stock because the current system of licensing is not based on reliable knowledge of existing stock.

The SFYP projects an annual increase in industrial output by 3% only, although it predicts very high growth rates for manufacturing, construction and public utilities. The expected low contribution of the sector was based on the assumption of stagnation in oil value-added during 2001-2005. This assumption, however, needs to be revised in the light of new projections of oil production with higher expected production levels during 2001-2003 and sharper declines during 2004-2005. Despite huge proven reserves of gas, the potentials of gas exports are unlikely to be tapped during the SFYP due to lack of secured external markets and financial resources. Similarly, the country's rich mining reserves are not expected to be fully utilized because of security concerns, conflicts over land ownership and poor infrastructure. While oil industry is still dominant, there is no evidence of a Dutch disease problem in Yemen but the GoY needs to be careful about the implications of decline in oil revenues in future.

Manufacturing in Yemen —characterized by high degree of industrial and geographical concentration, family ownership and low value-added to inputs ratio— remains a small sector. It contributed only 9% of GDP in the 1990s and its contribution to merchandise exports has been even weaker. The protectionist policies pursued until mid-1990s contributed to the fragility and inefficiency of the sector. However, macroeconomic stability, trade liberalization and reform of the exchange rate regime since mid-1990s started to have a positive impact on the sector. The SFYP targets an annual growth rate of manufacturing value-added of more than 9% and seeks to encourage exports of manufactures and development of small-scale industries. The realization of these targets, however, largely depends on removal of the constraints in the sector (high production costs, lack of technical skills, smuggling and dumping, lack of access to credit, *etc.*), further trade liberalization, improvements in infrastructure and utilities and strengthening the legal and judicial systems.

Services remained by far the largest contributor to GDP; constituting half GDP in the 1990s. Despite its dominance in total output, the growth rate of the sector lagged behind other sectors recording an average growth rate of 5.0% and its contribution to GDP growth was less commensurate to its relative size in GDP. Services are dominated by government services followed by transportation and communications, domestic trade, and real estate services. Services value-added is projected to increase by 8% per annum and to raise its contribution in GDP from 39% in 2000 to 43% by 2005. The plan puts heavy emphasis on tourism, transport and communications, and financial services. Yemen has huge potentials in tourism (e.g., historical, religious and archeological sites, coasts and islands, mountains and deserts) and tourism has been identified by the SFYP as one of the most promising sectors to accelerate GDP growth, increase rates of job creation and consequently assist in poverty alleviation efforts (targeted to grow annually by 11%). The attainment of this target may be difficult in the current circumstances and the increase in international business traffic is projected to rise by slightly more than the GDP growth rate and international vacation tourism to increase by up to three folds if the constraints affecting the sector are removed.

Properly executed infrastructure investment (including by the public sector) would be an important source of economic growth in Yemen, given the current weak state of basic infrastructure. In particular, the potentials for growth in the transport and communications sector are also large and the current condition of the networks and the high cost of services represent major hindrances to economic activities and initiatives. Despite liberalization and deregulation efforts, the whole sector remained largely under control of state (or private) monopolies and the government also controls most of the tariffs and fares. The sector should be accorded a higher priority because of its impact on other sectors.

THE AGRICULTURAL SECTOR

In Yemen, agricultural output is derived from two main sub-sectors: (i) fisheries; and, (ii) other agricultural activities including farming, forestry, livestock and Qat farming.[17] More than 93% of agriculture value added is contributed by the farming, forestry and livestock sub-sectors (of which about a third is Qat production) and the contribution of fishery to total agriculture value added was about 6.7% in the 1990s (1.3% of total GDP). Farming and

---

[17]   Qat is a stimulant leaf chewed on a daily basis by most Yemeni adults. Qat leaves contain three alcoholides: cathine, cathinine and cathidine as well as sugars, tannins and Vitamin C. The WHO considers Qat to have amphetamine-like properties and categorizes it as a separate drug group in which it is the sole element.

fishing activities are largely market-oriented, with production privately undertaken by farmers, though encouraged by the government and cooperatives in the provision of subsidized inputs.

The agricultural sector plays an important role in the Yemeni economy, not because of its contribution to GDP —though small and declining— but also because it provides employment to more than half of the labor force, livelihood to more than three quarters of population, and contributes about a third of total non-oil merchandize exports. The importance of the sector also stems from the fact that it utilizes between 90% and 93% of total water resources in Yemen. The continuing discrepancy between the low contribution of agriculture to GDP and the percentage of those employed in the sector (54% of total employment), reflects seasonal employment, underemployment and the low productivity of workers and of the factors of production; thus resulting in low incomes and poor standard of living for workers employed in the sector.

TABLE 2.1: AGRICULTURAL VALUE-ADDED, 1990-2005

	Share of GDP (%)				Average Annual Growth Rate (%)			
			End-FFYP	Target End-SFYP	Actual	Target FFYP	Actual FFYP	Target SFYP
	1990	1995	2000	2005	1990-1995	1996-2000	1996-2000	2001-2005
Farming, Livestock & Forestry (incl. Qat)	23.6	17.7	14.2	14.5	3.0	7.0	5.4	6.1
Qat	8.5	5.4	4.2	..	2.4	..	2.3	..
Farming, Livestock & Forestry (excl. Qat)	15.1	12.3	10.0	..	3.4	..	6.9	..
Fisheries	0.6	1.7	1.1	1.6	-1.6	7.0	12.3	13.0
Total Agricultural Value-Added	24.2	19.4	15.3	16.1	2.9	7.0	5.5	6.7

Sources: Central Statistical Organization (CSO) for 1990-2000, First Five-Year Plan (FFYP) for targets during 1996-2000, and the Second Five-Year Plan (SFYP) for 2001-2005.

As a whole, the agricultural sector was dynamic and contributed to GDP growth more than its relative share in GDP (especially in 1992, 1993 and 1998) but the sector's output has been very vulnerable to shortfalls in rainfall. Second, the relative importance of the agricultural sector in total output continued to decline in the 1990s from about a quarter in 1990 to about one-sixth of GDP by the 2000. This came about as a result of slow growth in the early 1990s following the 1990-1991 drought. Agricultural output declined by more than 7% in 1991 and recovered by 19% the following year due to exceptional rainfall. Agricultural output declined again in 1994 due to low precipitations. Third, agricultural value-added grew by 5.4% during the FFYP although the target growth rate of the plan was set at 7% per annum. Performance was assisted by the gradual removal of bans and controls, price liberalization, privatization of some agricultural units and improvements in storage and transportation facilities. All agricultural activities (excluding Qat) also showed impressive growth rates during 1996-2000 (Table 2.1).

The SFYP sets ambitious growth targets for the agricultural sector with an average annual growth rate of 6.7%; to reach higher levels of food security and agricultural exports mainly through productivity increases. It also aims to increase income of farmers to improve living standards, reduce poverty and underemployment in the sector. Higher growth targets are planned for fisheries. The major policy problems in the agriculture sector include under-pricing of water and the rapid depletion of aquifers (also due to subsidies in diesel prices and electricity tariffs), lack of data and controls on the fish stocks and poor infrastructure resulting in low productivity in the sector.

Fisheries

Yemen is endowed with rich fish resources including surface and deep-water fish, shrimp and other shellfish. Due to the use of intensive labor in typical fishing activities, the availability of warm waters throughout the year, and the nutrient rich upwelling systems, fisheries are considered among the most promising sectors by the Strategic Vision 2025 and the SFYP for job creation, income generation and export potentials. The long coastal strip —extending over 2,000 km— the widespread islands and territorial waters in the Red and Arabian seas and the Gulf of Aden, provide significant fisheries resources and various forms of marine life that will enable the sector to contribute effectively to the implementation of the Food Security Strategy of Yemen. [18]

Fisheries sector developed differently in the two former republics before unification. In the PDRY, the government focused on industrial foreign and state-owned fisheries in the Gulf of Aden while in the YAR the government gradually and successfully developed small-scale fisheries in the Red Sea. In the early 1990s, fishing was protected by import bans and controls on exports. Since 1994, the GoY has allowed large foreign industrial fleets to return to its water under bilateral agreements and individual licensing schemes. About 113 licensed foreign vessels and unknown numbers of unlicensed vessels are currently exploiting the fish stock and are increasing the risk of collapse of the entire stock while hampering the development of small-scale fishing.

The contribution of fisheries to total GDP was only 1.1% in 2000 and throughout the 1990s its impact on GDP growth was very weak.[19] Between 1990 and 1995, fisheries value-added declined by an annual average of 1.6%. Some of the controls were removed in mid-1990s and activity picked up. Value-added of the fisheries achieved an average growth rate of 12.3% during the FFYP (1.1% of GDP) versus a target of 7.0% per annum. However, the sub-sector has the potential to grow rapidly so as to increase its share up to 5% of GDP (provided that the stock remains sustainable), enhance protein consumption, promote agricultural exports, and raise personal income from small and medium-size fisheries.[20] The SFYP estimates that the fish reserves amount to 850,000 tons, which would allow for annual production ranging from 350,000–400,000 tons, as compared to 135,000 tons utilized in 2000. The sector is planned to grow at a faster rate of 13.0% during 2001-2005, raising the volume of output to 248,000 tons by 2005. The plan also targets an increase in fish exports by an annual average rate of 11.5% to reach 38,000 tons by 2005.

Resources, Potentials, and Constraints in the Fisheries Sub-Sector

Yemen has considerable demersal and pelagic fish resources. Annual fish catch was between 70,000 and 120,000 tons in the 1990s and is estimated to have reached 135,000 tons in 2000; of which 70% is by small-scale fisheries and the rest is high value fish by licensed and unlicensed industrial vessels. Yemen's most valuable fish stock (rock lobster, cuttlefish, shrimp and bottom-dwelling species) can potentially yield close to US$ 100 million annually of which about 50% could be exported. Cuttlefish exports could grow from the current

---

[18] For a detailed review of fish resources in Yemen, see World Bank (1999; 3-5).
[19] Fisheries made a big impact on GDP growth only in 1991 and 1994 when the sector grew by more than 50% and 100%, respectively (see Annex Table 3).
[20] World Bank (1999) and Barrès (2001).

1,500 tons to a potential of 5,000-8,000 tons (US$ 15-25 million) annually. Shrimp resources could grow from the current 500-800 tons to a potential of 500-1,400 tons (US$ 6 million) annually. Rock lobster could contribute to 400-600 tons (US$ 5-9 million) annually, while current official exports are around US$ 1.5 million.[21]

The status of fisheries resources is unknown because of the absence of proper scientific research and lack of reliable statistics, especially for the stocks facing over-exploitation. Since 1991, no dependable fish landing statistics have been collected (specially for the small-scale fleet) and no reliable resource surveys, stock assessment and catch statistics are available. The current system of licensing is not based on reliable knowledge of standing stocks and, therefore, it may be dangerously contributing to the over-exploitation of the fish stocks. Although there is little disagreement between local and foreign scientists about the heavy exploitation of fish stocks, disagreement exists about the impact of current fishing levels on resources and the level of risk of stock collapses. Similarly, views differ about the desirability of the current licensing regime and its objectives. It is difficult to assess the political benefits of the bilateral agreements against their potential negative impact on small-scale fisheries. However, the concerns expressed by local and foreign scientists and fishery specialists about the state of the stocks should be taken very seriously and the "cautionary principle" developed by FAO should be applied. Although Yemen's own industrial fleet developed during the PDRY no longer functions for lack of maintenance and management, fish resources are heavily over-exploited by foreign licensed and unlicensed industrial fleets.

The key constraints that are currently inhibiting growth of the fisheries sector and its contribution to economic growth and job creation include: (i) poor fish resources management and the imbalances between industrial and small-scale fisheries; (ii) poor institutional performance; (iii) lack of critical infrastructure in selected areas; (iv) poor fish marketing and lack of effective quality controls; and (v) lack of institutional and physical infrastructure to support aquaculture development.

Farming, Forestry, Livestock, and Qat

Yemen is divided in four agro-ecological zones: the Highlands (44% of cultivated area and 61% of the farms), the Eastern Plateau (26% of the area, 19% of the farms), the Tihama (26% of the area, 10% of the farms) and the Coastal Area (Gulf of Aden, with 4% of the area, 10% of the farms). About two thirds of cultivable land is currently under cultivation. Again, slightly less than two-thirds of cultivated land is cropped by cereals, 15% by fruits and vegetables, 10% by livestock grass and 9% by the Qat trees. About 53% of cultivated area is rain-fed, 30% is irrigated by ground water and streams and spate irrigation irrigate the rest. The livestock sector represents about a quarter of agriculture value-added and grew by an average rate of 4.8% during the FFYP.

The main features of agriculture in Yemen are the low productivity and the substantial yield gap for most crops. For many crops the current yields are well below technical potential and actual farmers yield in comparable countries.[22] Furthermore, post

---

21   Barrès (2001).
22   Barrès (2001) shows that the yield gap can be as high as 40% for potato and tomato, 60% for banana, and 20% for oranges.

harvest losses are estimated to be quite high (20% for cereals, 45% for tomato, 60% for papaya, and 38% for banana). The main causes are harvesting techniques, rough handling and poor packaging and weaknesses in transport networks.

TABLE 2.2: AGRICULTURAL LAND IN YEMEN BY MAJOR CROPS

	Area (hectares)	Ratio of total Cultivated land (%)
Total Cultivable Land	1,668,858	--
Cultivated Area	1,132,910	100
Total Cereals	675,394	60
Wheat	86,112	8
Other Cereals	589,480	52
Vegetables	62,498	6
Cash Crops (without Qat)	93,086	8
Fruit	88,104	8
Fodder Grass	114,197	10
Qat	99,631	9

Source: Computed from Table 1-3 of the Second Five-Year Plan (SFYP, 2001).

Qat and Water Resources: The Two Major Constraints in the Sector

In 2001, Qat contributed 4.2% of GDP, 28.7% of total agricultural value-added, and absorbed about a quarter of agricultural work-force and a tenth of household income. It is exclusively cultivated in the Highlands (73% of total Qat cultivations and 75% of cash crop area in the zone) and in the Eastern Plateau. Although Qat covers 9% of total cultivated area, its plantation is increasing rapidly (36% rise over cultivated area in 1989), particularly in Sana'a, Ibb, Hajjah and Dhamar governorates. It is more likely that Qat cultivation will continue to increase because it is more profitable in comparison with other crops under the same conditions and given the rise in the demand for Qat consumption. This will in turn exert more pressure on limited ground-water resources and increase rates of displacement of other crops such as grapes, coffee and cereals.

BOX 2.1: TOWARD AN AGENDA FOR QAT

The SFYP courageously addressed the Qat issue in Yemen. The GoY also has recently carried out an extended study on Qat and its findings were discussed in a national conference in April 2002.

The following observations could be among the agenda for future discussions on Qat issues:

- Although environmental, medical and social reasons calls for a reduction in Qat production, the high profitability of Qat and the lack of attractive alternative crops for rural small-scale farmers, makes the reduction in Qat cultivated areas highly unrealistic in the short-term;
- In the short-term, the objective of the GoY should be to stabilize the area under Qat cultivation through: (a) increasing Qat yield per hectare; (b) promoting water saving irrigation techniques; (c) increasing the profitability of other competing crops (grapes, vegetables and fruits and coffee); and, (d) promoting public awareness on the heath and social impacts of Qat, as a follow-up to the recent Qat Conference;
- In the medium-term, public awareness on the negative effects of Qat should progressively reduce demand for Qat and profitable alternatives will be developed;
- In the Highlands, Qat would continue to play a major role in poverty reduction in the marginal upper catchments, where access is difficult and costly, where land and economic opportunities are very limited, and where Qat is either rainfed or irrigated from shallow aquifers.

Source: Barrès (2001)

Limited water resources is the major constraint for expansion in agricultural production. Between 1970 and 2000, irrigated agriculture had tripled from 210,000 hectare to 630,000 hectare. Located within a dry and semi-arid area, Yemen is among the world poorest countries in water resources. Per capita share of recoverable water resources amounts to 137 m^3 in comparison with 1,250 m^3 for the MENA region, 7,500 m^3 world wide, while the water poverty line is estimated at 1,000 m³. Average annual rainfall ranges from 500-800 mm in the highlands, 50-100 mm in the coastal areas and less than 50 mm in eastern governorates. Water sustainability started to worsen in the 1970s with the digging of deep tube wells (about 50,000 wells) for both drinking and agricultural use, subsidization of diesel prices and water and electricity tariffs. These resulted in depletion of groundwater, particularly in basins of western governorates (e.g., Sana'a, Sa'ada and Taiz basins).

The gap between available water resources (2.5 billion m³) and the current water uses (estimated at 3.4 billion m³) has increased from 400 million m³ in 1990 to 900 million m³ in 2000 and is predicted to reach 1.0 billion m³ by 2010 (with the assumption of increased efficiency in water use). With this trend, it is expected that 12 billion m³ of the estimated 20 billion m³ of ground water reserves will be depleted by 2010.[23] In addition to the depletion of groundwater resources (about 4 meters per annum), quality of water is also threatened by pollution, petroleum wastes, fertilizers and pesticides and rise in salinity, which makes it non–potable even for use in agriculture. Furthermore, returns on water are also very low due to low efficiency of irrigation systems. It is estimated that losses between the well and the field ranged from 9% to 78%, and in more than two thirds of cases, the losses exceeded 30%. Therefore, the growth prospects for crops, which rely on irrigation from ground water, would be seriously constrained by the sustainability of water resources.

Water sustainability in Yemen is affected mainly by inefficient pricing of water, electricity and diesel as well as acquiring pumps at concessional prices. This is partly due to lack of clarification on organization and ownership of water assets. For instance, Qat growers usually do not own the aquifers they use nor do they pay any fees or charges for such use. They pump water using subsidized electricity and diesel. As a result of this rapid mining, large parts of the rural economy could disappears within a generation. Public institutions dealing with water have not been efficient.[24] A draft Water Law will be approved by the Parliament soon and is expected to play an important role in sustaining water uses and clarification of water rights and property.

Other constraints which hamper the development of the agricultural sector include; (i) high prices on niche markets and lack of quality controls which hamper competitiveness of agricultural exports, (ii) decline in traditional rain-fed agriculture and livestock systems as a result of rapid growth of the irrigated sector, (iii) deterioration of the upper catchments which have been neglected by past infrastructure projects leading to degradation of age-old systems of terracing and water harvesting.

Growth Potentials of Non-Fishery Agricultural Sector

The growth target for the agricultural sector of 6.7% over the SFYP seems rather high by historical trends and the experience of other countries. The target is high because of higher growth target set for fisheries. Excluding fisheries, the growth target for farming, livestock and Qat that is set at 6.1% during 2001-2005 and can be achieved if the constraints in the sector are addressed. Table 2.3 illustrates how this target can be achieved if the non-

---

23   SFYP (2001; 26).
24   For water shortages, sustainability, and policy problems, see World Bank (1997).

Qat cultivated areas are increased, increase in Qat plantations is arrested, and extension services and irrigation techniques are improved.

TABLE 2.3: A SCENARIO FOR INCREASED AGRICULTURAL VALUE-ADDED

	Value of Production in 2000 Prices	Annual Increase in Cultivated Area (%)	Annual Increase in Yields (%)	Combined Annual Growth Rates
Cereals	169	0	5	5.0
Qat	636	0	3	3.0
Other Cash Crops	88	3	6	9.2
Vegetables & Fruits	513	3	6	9.2
Pulses	30	5	5	10.3
Total	1,425			6.0

Source: Barrès (2001).

First, rain-fed cereals have the potential to grow by up to 12% per annum with improved quality of indigenous seeds and better crop husbandry. Second, irrigated crops (vegetables and fruits) have the potential to grow by up to 16% annually with improved extension services and better management of irrigation (Box 2.2). Third, livestock has good potentials for growth with improved husbandry practices, cross breeding and improved management of rangelands.[25]

BOX 2.2: EXPORTS OF COFFEE, FRUIT, AND VEGETABLES

Yemen's coffee export is the third largest export item and it totaled US$ 34.3 million in 1999. Accordingly, Yemen is ranked the 41st largest coffee exporter with a 0.3% share in the world coffee market, despite Yemen having a world famous coffee variety (Mocha). Coffee exports performed well in the 1990s, thanks to lower depreciation in price of Arabica coffee relative to prices for other blends. Price of Arabica coffee depreciated by 42% less than the average coffee price, which declined by 48% from 1995 to 1999. Coffee exports grew faster during 1994-1999 with an annual average of 19%, far faster than Brazil (8.5%) and world coffee market (7.6%) during the same period.

Yemen's coffee market is highly concentrated with Saudi Arabia representing 85% of total coffee exports (US$ 29 million in 1999). Although Yemen is a top coffee exporter to Saudi Arabia (satisfying 30% of Saudi domestic coffee market), Yemen's share in the GCC coffee market is still the fourth (9.2% of market share) following Ethiopia (37%), India (13%) and Spain (12%). Coffee exports to the GCC have strong potentials in the short- and medium-terms.

Fruits and vegetables are among the fastest growing export item in Yemen. They increased from US$ 0.1 million in 1994 to US$ 12.3 million in 1999. Currently, exports of fruits and vegetables account for 0.5% of total exports and 9% of non-oil exports. Traditionally, the main export market for fruits and vegetable is Saudi Arabia (99.2% of total exports of fruits and vegetables in 1999). Yemen is ranked the 17th largest fruit and vegetable exporter to Saudi Arabia and rapidly improved its market position in Saudi's fruit and vegetable market from 0.01% in 1991, to 0.2% in 1995, and to 1.6% in 1999. Banana is the largest item in Yemen's fruit and vegetable export to Saudi Arabia (US$ 4.5 million in 1999 and 7.2% of Saudi's total banana imports).

Source: Someya (2001).

THE INDUSTRIAL SECTOR

Despite its relatively small contribution to GDP, the performance of the industrial sector was very impressive throughout the 1990s. During 1990-1995, the sector managed to record a 5.5% average annual growth rate, mainly due to high growth rates of the oil and mining sectors (6.1%) while total manufacturing value-added grew by 5.0%, construction by 4.6% and utilities by 3.1%. During the FFYP, performance of the whole sector improved further with an annul growth rate of 6.5%. Again, oil and mining was among the fastest growing sub-sectors (7.6%), following the 12.7% growth rate of construction sub-sector,

---

[25]   For details on the potential of various crops, see on Barrès (2001) and FAO (2001).

while manufacturing (excluding refining) grew by 3.1%, utilities by 6.0% and oil refining declined by an annul average rate of 1.4% (Table2.4).

TABLE 2.4: INDUSTRIAL VALUE-ADDED, 1990-2005 (%)

	Share of GDP				Growth Rate			
			End-FFYP	Target End-SFYP	Actual	Target FFYP	Actual FFYP	Target SFYP
	1990	1995	2000	2005	1990-1995	1996-2000	1996-2000	2001-2005
1. Oil, Mining and Quarrying	13.6	13.8	33.8	25.8	6.1	0.6	7.6	0.04
Mining and Quarrying	0.2	0.3	0.1	0.1	3.3	..	1.5	10.0
Oil & Gas	13.4	13.5	33.7	25.7	6.1	..	7.7	0.0
2. Manufacturing	9.3	14.3	7.5	8.8	5.0	8.0	2.4	9.2
Manufacturing ex. Refining	7.3	12.6	4.9	6.0	6.2	..	3.1	10.0
Oil Refining	2.0	1.7	2.6	2.8	0.0	..	-1.4	7.5
3. Water, Gas, Electricity	1.2	0.6	0.7	0.8	3.1	4.0	6.0	9.2
4. Construction & Building	2.7	3.5	4.2	5.5	4.6	8.0	12.7	11.0
Total Industrial Value Added	**26.8**	**32.2**	**46.2**	**40.9**	**5.5**	**4.0**	**6.5**	**3.04**

.. : Not available

Source : Central Statistical Organization (CSO) for 1990-2000, FFYP for targets for 1996-2000, and the SFYP for 2001-2005.

The SFYP makes very conservative predictions for the growth of the industrial sector (3.0%) as a result of low targets set for the oil sector. However, the plan targets very high growth rates for mining (10%), manufacturing (10%), utilities (9.2%) and construction (10%). Chapter 5 summarizes the constraints and potentials of these subs-sectors, the feasibility of these growth targets in the light of the identified constraints and potentials, and the suggested policies and reform measures to tap these potentials. The following sections provide a detailed review of the most important sub-sectors: gas, mining, and manufacturing which are identified by the SFYP as promising sectors in addition to the oil sector given its current relative importance and its impact on other economic sectors.

The Oil Sector

Yemen is a small player in the oil market with small proven reserves and production levels. Although exploration work started in the 1930s, it was not until 1970s that serious exploration work started and about 18 agreements were signed with oil companies for exploration and production.[26] Actual oil production started in the mid-1980s and currently there are six producing blocks in Yemen (Shabwah, Marib, Masila, Jannah, Ayad and Hawarim).

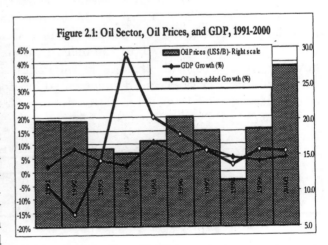

Figure 2.1: Oil Sector, Oil Prices, and GDP, 1991-2000

By the end of 2000, Yemen's remaining recoverable reserves stood at 2.8 billion barrels. Unless new discoveries are made, oil production is expected to decrease by an annual average of 3-5% because some oil fields started to dry up.[27]

---

[26]   IMF (2001; 11). Most agreements specified 20% share for cost oil and the profit sharing was on average 20% for the company and 80% for the government.

[27]   About 0.03 billion barrels in Hawarim, 0.11 billion barrels in Ayad, 0.18 billion barrels in Shabwah, 0.28 billion barrels in Jannah, 0.413 billion barrels in Marib, and 1.41 billion barrels in Masila. Other exploration blocks (S1, S2, 9 and 15) added about 0.38 billion barrels to recoverable reserves. These reserves can be

First, Total of France discovered oil in the Shabwah field (block 10) in 1986 and production was limited to 10,000 b/d due to uncompleted facilities. Oil was trucked from the field to the Aden refinery. Currently the field produces 285,000 b/d. Second, a major field in Marib (block 18) started production in 1987 and a pipeline exported most of its output. Production in Marib fields reached 112,000 b/d in 2001. Third, the Masila field (block 14) —operated by Canadian Occidental— started production in 1993 (40,000 b/d). A pipeline to the Indian Ocean was completed in 1994 when production increased to 150,000 b/d and production increased further to about 231,000 b/d in 2001. Fourth, another consortium of companies started exploration in Jannah block (block 5) in 1990. Production started in 1996 with 4,000 b/d and reached 58,000 in 2001. Fifth, Nimir Petroleum signed an exploration agreement for the Ayad block in 1991. Currently the field produces only 4,500 b/d. Finally, Hawarim (Block 36) field operated by the DNO of Norway came on stream in 2000 and its production reached 8,200 b/d in 2001. Furthermore, exploration blocks were awarded in the last four years and the financial incentives for oil companies were improved.[28]

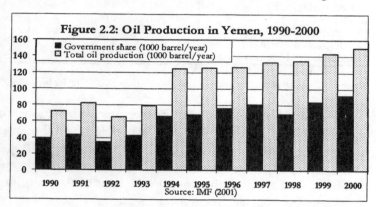

Source: World Bank, Live Database (LDB), 2001.

Half of the industrial output in Yemen in the 1990s was constituted by oil and mining (averaging 13% of GDP during 1990-2000). The contribution of oil was, however, very volatile mainly due to changes in oil prices and to some extent due to fluctuations in annual production levels. Oil production increased steadily in the 1990s from 72 million barrels in 1990 (198,340 b/d) to 150 million barrels (410,452 b/d) in 2000. Oil value-added, however, fluctuated with changes in oil prices. It declined by 10% during 1991-1992, recovered to 4% in 1993, and then increased by more than 25% during 1994-1996. Collapse of oil prices in 1997-1998, led to a growth rate of less than 5% before the sector resumed its high growth in 1999-2000 averaging 7.5%.

TABLE 2.5: OIL FISCAL REVENUES, 1990-2000

	1990	1991	1992	1993	1994	1995	1996	1997	1998	1999	2000
Oil and Gas Revenues (YR billions)	8.3	17	8	10	11	28	135	190	118	206	446
As % of Total Revenues	34	44	23	26	26	31	61	66	52	61	76
As % of GDP	6.6	11.0	4.0	4.0	3.5	5.5	18.1	21.4	13.8	18.2	32.3

Sources: Computed from Data from Ministry of Finance, 2001.

The impact of oil on economic growth, fiscal revenues and export proceedings continued to increase rapidly in the 1990s. The share of oil in GDP declined from 13% in 1990 to 5.4% in 1993. It then started to increase gradually in 1994 (6% of GDP) reaching 28% in 1997. A sharp decline occurred in 1998 (16.2%) but it then started to rise again

---

exhausted in 18 years at current production levels. However, the SFYP estimates proven reserves at 5.7 billion barrels. According to most recent figures this could be overestimation of reserves or it did not take into account withdrawal from the reserves throughout the 1990s.

[28]   By 2000, more than 26 oil companies were conducting exploration work in 30 blocks [IMF (2001: 8-16)].

reaching 29% in 1999 and peaking at 34% of GDP in 2000.[29] Reliance on oil as the main source of fiscal revenues also increased in the late 1990s from 25% of fiscal revenues during 1992-1994 to 76% of fiscal revenues in 2000 (Table 2.5). The contribution of oil sector to total employment is very limited in Yemen. Total Yemeni workers in the sector have reached 18,000 in 2002, of which more than 12,000 are employed in the Ministry of Oil and Minerals and its associated units. Employment in the oil companies is about 2,800 and in the oil services is about 2,800 (see Annex Table 17).

The government exports two-thirds of its oil share while companies export their entire share (averaged 43% of total production in the late 1990s). Oil exports increased from US$ 1.2 billion in 1990 (78% of merchandise exports) to US$ 2.3 billion in 1997 (90% of merchandise exports). It declined in 1998 to US$ 2.2 billion and recovered to US$ 2.7 billion in 1999 before peaking in 2000 at US$ 3.7 billion (96% of merchandise exports). In 1999, Yemen was ranked the 32nd largest oil exporter with 0.7% market share. Oil exports account for more than 90% of total exports, which is second highest, only next to Iraq, among 230 countries in the world.[30] Yemen's oil export markets are also highly concentrated. The top five oil export markets account for 87% of Yemen's oil exports compared to 53% for Iran, 61% for Saudi Arabia, and 73% for UAE and Nigeria. Moreover, all the top five destinations (Thailand, China, Korea, India and Singapore) are emerging markets. Being a new oil exporter, Yemen was targeted as a new source of oil supply by those rapidly growing Asian economies which had high demands for oil but faced an already established international oil supply system dominated by international oil cartel. As a consequence, East Asian countries are now major oil importers from Yemen. However, the heavy concentration of oil export markets and heavy dependence on emerging markets imply vulnerability to oil prices as well as external shocks.

Despite the dominance of the oil industry in Yemen's economy in the 1990s, there is no evidence that there is a Dutch-disease problem (see also Chapter 3) or that the oil dominance suppressed economic growth in the rest of the economy. Yemen is still very far from full employment and there are no indications that prices of non-tradables have risen excessively. Second, real wages declined significantly over the past decade. Third, the adoption of the floating exchange rate regime in 1996 resulted in a significant depreciation of the real effective exchange rate (REER) in 1996-97 and ensured its stability in the following four years. Finally, as shown in Chapter 1, non-oil GDP growth in the late 1990s was much better than in the early 1990s.

Implications of Expected Decline in Production, 2001-2020

Oil production is expected to decline by an annual average of 11% during 2001-2010 if no new recoverable reserves are discovered, with sharper declines during 2005-2010. Total oil production reached 159 million barrels in 2000 with the government share reaching 61% of total production. With expected decline in oil prices in the short- and long-terms, government share of oil production is also expected to decline because of the treatment of

---

[29] Yemen has also two refineries. Aden refinery was constructed in 1954 with an initial capacity of 150,000 b/d. Capacity declined to 110,000 b/d in 1990 and further to 70,000 after the damage caused by the war in 1994. Marib refinery was constructed in 1986 with a capacity of 10,000 b/d for domestic consumption.

[30] This figure is extremely high in comparison with other oil exporters such as Saudi Arabia (12.5% of world oil exports and 80% oil export ratio) and Indonesia (1.6% world market share and oil export ratio of 9.5%).

"cost oil" in the agreements with oil companies. With falling oil prices, the share of companies increases to recover costs of exploration and production.

TABLE 2.6: PROJECTED OIL PRODUCTION BY THE SECOND FIVE-YEAR PLAN (SFYP)
(thousand barrels per day)

	2000	2001	2002	2003	2004	2005
Production from Current Recoverable and Confirmed Reserves	436,000	425,100	414,473	404,111	394,008	384,158
Output from the Expected New Discoveries	-	65,400	137,340	216,678	304,380	401,528
Total	436,000	490,500	551,813	620,789	698,388	785,686

Source: Derived from data in the Second Five-Year Plan (SFYP; 2001).

The SFYP aims to maintain the same level of real oil value-added by increasing production from new fields to compensate for the expected decline in production from existing fields. It assumes no real growth in oil output during 2000-2005 and as a result the share of oil in total GDP is predicted to decline from about a third to about one-fourth. This projection was based on two assumptions: (i) an annual decline in oil production from existing fields by 2.5%, and (ii) an increase in total oil production as a result of new discoveries amounting to an annual increase in oil production in 2000 by 12.5%.[31] Therefore, the SFYP predicts an annual increase in total oil production of about 10% in the next five years.[32] The SFYP predicts that oil prices during the last four years of the plan will be in the range of US$ 18-25 per barrel (Table 2.6).

TABLE 2.7: REVISED PROJECTIONS FOR OIL PRODUCTION, 2001-2010

	Total Average Production (thousands of barrels per day	Total Annual Production (millions of barrels per year)	Annual Growth Rate (%)
2000	436	159	
2001	440	161	0.9
2002	448	163	1.8
2003	417	152	-6.9
2004	378	138	-9.3
2005	343	125	-9.3
2006	290	106	-15.5
2007	238	87	-17.9
2008	198	72	-16.8
2009	170	62	-14.2
2010	143	52	-15.6

Source: Data obtained from the Ministry of Oil and Minerals (December 2001).

Revised estimates from the Ministry of Oil and Minerals indicate that the assumptions used by the SFYP were pessimistic with regard to production levels from existing oil fields. Based on these new estimates, oil production increased in 2001 (440,000 b/d) and is projected to increase further in 2002 (448,000 b/d). In the following years, unless production from new fields is added, oil production is projected to decline rapidly by 7% in 2003, and 9% in 2004 (378,00 b/d) and 2005 (343,000 b/d). Oil production from producing fields will decline more sharply during 2005-2010 (Table 2.7). Thus, it seems that the projections of the SFYP for oil value-added are on the low side for 2001-2003 and on the high side for 2004-2005. Assuming: (i) oil production as predicted in Table 2.7; (ii) no additional production from new fields; (iii) GDP growth as envisaged by the plan at 5.6%

---

[31] For instance, oil production from sector 53 (east of Masar) is expected to start in 2002.

[32] These forecasts are different from the conservative predictions of the FFYP, which forecasted an annual decline in oil production from 344,000 b/d in 1995 to 331,000 b/d in 2000. However, actual oil production increased by an average annual rate of 4.9% until it reached 436,000 b/d in 2000.

per annum; (iv) oil prices as projected by the World Bank Global Economic Prospects; and, (v) exchange rates as projected by the World Bank LDB, the share of oil to total GDP is likely to continue to decline to 31% in 2001, 27% in 2002, 24% in 2003, 20% in 2004 and to 16% in 2005. Given the uncertainty about prospects of oil prices and oil production in these forecasts, these projections should be interpreted as preliminary and tentative.

Gas and Mining

The gas sector in Yemen is estimated to have reserves of about 12-15 trillion cubic feet.[33] Currently, about 95% of the produced gas is re-injected into the ground because of the delay in the Natural Gas Export project, which is now expected to start in 2005. The inability to find external markets is one of the most significant problems facing the development and improvement of the gas sector, especially in light of strong competition from affluent countries in the Gulf and the scarce financing resources available for Yemen's gas export projects. However, gas production for domestic use is expected to increase, particularly for the Marib power station, which is expected to start its operations in 2003. Currently, domestic consumption is met with about 30,000 b/d equivalent of liquefied natural gas (LNG) from the Marib block. In addition to the importance of gas as a clean source of energy, it can also be an important source of foreign currencies if Yemen manages to export it. Gas can also be an essential input for a number of petrochemical applications and industries. However, it is unlikely that natural gas will have a significant impact on economic growth during the course of implementing the SFYP.

TABLE 2.8: IMPORTANT FIELDS IN MINERAL EXPLORATIONS IN YEMEN

Raw Material Type	Reserves	Number of Locations
Lime Stone and Dolomite	10 billion m³	32
Gypse	160 million ton	14
Marble	690 million m³	12
Volcanic Glass:		13
Bio-mass	34.5 million m³	
Burlit	300 million m³	
Granite	316 million m³	25
Building Stones:		15
Tuff	31 million m³	
Basalt	58 million m³	
Desert Salt	337 million ton	11
Glass Sand	157 million m³	11

Source: SFYP (2001).

Recent surveying, exploring and excavating for minerals have led to the discovery of promising reserves such as gold in Hajjah, platinum in Amran, titanium in Abyan, in addition to other important mineral reserves such as limestone, gypsum, marble, rock salt, granite stone and basalt (Table 2.8). The SFYP aims to increase value-added of mining and quarrying by 10% per annum. This is unlikely to be met unless the GoY addresses four major constraints, namely: (i) security concerns in areas with mining reserves;[34] (ii) poor infrastructure which makes some of the areas inaccessible; (iii) lack of incentives and

---

[33]   IMF (2001; 22) shows that most of the proven reserves are in the Marib field (13.5 trillion cubic feet), 2 trillion cubic feet in Block S1 and the rest in the Jannah field.
[34]   A number of companies pulled out of the sector because of increasing security threats, tribal conflicts, and lack of clear laws and regulations to organize land ownership and utilization of natural resources.

promotions to attract FDI into the sector, and; (iv) ambiguity of laws and regulations with regard to land ownership and utilization of natural resources.

Manufacturing

Manufacturing activities in Yemen expanded in the early 1970s as a result of the momentum demand for consumer goods (fueled mainly by workers' remittances from the Gulf and foreign aid) and the government policies for granting economic incentives for local manufacturers using import substitution policies including protective measure such as tariffs, quantitative restrictions, price controls, and later by encouraging manufacturers for export production [World Bank (1989)]. Despite differences in the political and economic systems in the former republics, the public sector took the lead in manufacturing activities in both countries. In the PDRY, the government pursued the creation of a strong public sector to carry out all economic activities and nationalized most of private sector manufacturing establishments. In the YAR, although the private sector (local and foreign) was allowed to invest in manufacturing and played an important role in its development, manufacturing investments were driven mainly by the public sector.

Import substitution policies, pursued in the 1970s and the 1980s provided the necessary impetus for producing manufactured goods such as food products, footwear, clothing, leather products, drugs, and construction materials. Public sector manufacturing activities focused on large-scale projects such as cement, cotton, tobacco, drugs, petroleum, textiles, printing and, to some extent, food processing. The private sector concentrated its activities on food and beverage processing, building materials, woodwork, leather, soap production and light engineering.

Current Characteristics of Manufacturing Activities in Yemen

Recent surveying, exploring and excavating for minerals have led to the discovery of promising reserves such as gold in Hajjah, platinum in Amran, titanium in Abyan, in addition to other important mineral reserves such as limestone, gypsum, marble, rock salt, granite stone and basalt (Table 2.8). The SFYP aims to increase value-added of mining and quarrying by 10% per annum. This is unlikely to be met unless the GoY addresses four major constraints, namely: (i)

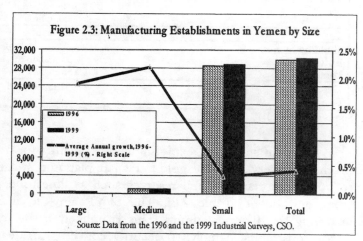

Figure 2.3: Manufacturing Establishments in Yemen by Size

Source: Data from the 1996 and the 1999 Industrial Surveys, CSO.

security concerns in areas with mining reserves;[35] (ii) poor infrastructure which makes some of the areas inaccessible; (iii) lack of incentives and promotions to attract FDI into the

---

[35]   A number of companies pulled out of the sector because of increasing security threats, tribal conflicts, and lack of clear laws and regulations to organize land ownership and utilization of natural resources.

sector, and; (iv) ambiguity of laws and regulations with regard to land ownership and utilization of natural resources.

Manufacturing sector is still a small part of the Yemeni economy despite expansion in the 1990s and its contribution to GDP, economic growth, exports and employment remains tiny.[36] The main characteristics of manufacturing activities in Yemen include: (i) small size of enterprises; (ii) high degree of industrial and geographical concentration; (iii) family and private ownership; (iv) a very low ratio of value-added to inputs (40%); and, (v) self-financing of investment and activities.

Total number of industrial establishments, which was 33,284 in 1996, increased to 33,699 in 1999, and was estimated at 33,972 by the end of 2000.[37] According to the 1999 Industrial Survey, the number of manufacturing establishments was 30,174. Of these, 1% were large establishments (more than 10 workers), 4% were medium-scale (4-9 workers) while the bulk (95%) of the manufacturing establishments were small-scale. In the second half of the 1990s, large and medium-scale establishments expanded more quickly than small-scale establishments (Figure 2.3).

TABLE 2.9: MANUFACTURING ESTABLISHMENTS BY SIZE AND ACTIVITY, 1999

	Large	Medium	Small	Total	% of Total Number
Food Processing	77	351	15,377	15,805	52.4
Textiles, Clothing & Leather	32	102	3,893	4,027	13.3
Wooden and Furniture	25	112	3,493	3,630	12.0
Miscellaneous Metal Products	45	189	3,238	3,472	11.5
Non-metallic (Construction)	34	271	2,748	3,053	10.1
Paper & Printing	31	36	29	96	0.3
Mechanisms and Equipment	7	18	21	46	0.2
Chemicals and Plastic	35	4	4	43	0.1
Oil Refinery	2	0	0	2	0.0

Source: CSO "Industrial Survey: 1999 Update" (2000).

Until 1999, more than half of all manufacturing establishments were in food processing. This was followed by textiles, clothing and leather (13%), woodwork and furniture (12%), non-metallic construction manufacturing (10%) and metal products. With regard to ownership of establishments, 99% of all manufacturing (and 67% of large) establishments were owned by private Yemeni citizens, 0.4% by the public sector (19% of large establishments), 0.3% by cooperatives, 0.4% were joint ventures and only 0.1% were owned by foreigners.[38] Furthermore, manufacturing activities were concentrated in a few governorates.[39] About a quarter of all manufacturing establishments were located in Sana'a, followed by Ibb (13%), Taiz (9%), Dhamar and Lahj (8% each) and Hodeidah (7%). These six governorates and the Capital secretariat hosted more than 71% of total manufacturing establishments in Yemen. Sana'a, Taiz and Hodeidah had also the largest concentration of large and medium-scale manufacturing establishments (Table 2.9).

---

[36] This section draws mainly on material in Al-Sabbry (2001) and Sherwood (2002).

[37] CSO (2000) "Statistical Year Book".

[38] For an extended review of manufacturing sector in Yemen, size, geographical distribution, type of activity, type of ownership, legal status, investments and capital stock, see Al-Sabbry (2001).

[39] Based on the 1996 Survey. The 1999 industrial survey did not have geographical distribution.

The manufacturing sector employed 95,413 workers in 1999 (2.5% of the 4.2 million total labor force),[40] mainly in food processing (40% of total manufacturing work force), followed by textiles, clothing and leather (14%), construction materials (13%), wood furniture and metal products (with 11% each). About 36% of employment in the sector takes place at large establishments, 7% at medium-scale establishments and 57% at small enterprises. Financial institutions contribute only marginally to the financing of manufacturing activities in Yemen. According to the 1996 survey, 99% of small and medium establishments were self-financed. For large establishments, owners financed 61% of activities from own resources, followed by joint ventures financing (26%) and the government with 11% (Figure 2.4).

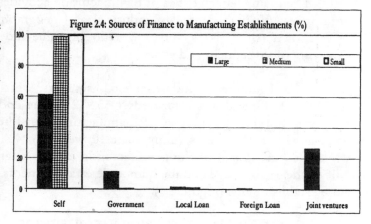

Figure 2.4: Sources of Finance to Manufactuing Establishments (%)

The total value added of manufacturing sector was YR 103 billion in 2000 (34% of which is oil refining), and mainly contributed by large establishments (67% of total manufacturing value-added), followed by small (29%) and medium (4%) establishments. The ratio of value-added to input is low and estimated at 40% in 1999 (with marked differences between large, medium and small establishments).[41] At the sectoral level, among the non-oil refining manufacturing, food products and beverages value-added was the highest (23% of total manufacturing value-added), followed by structural non-metallic products (13%), tobacco (12%), wood products (3%), paper, printing and publishing (4%), wood work and furniture (3%), metal products (3%) while the share of textiles declined to less than 1% of total manufacturing output.

Manufacturing Output, Contribution to Growth, and Exports in the 1990s

The low contribution of manufacturing sector to the economy can be traced to geographical and historical factors in addition to the protectionist policies adopted until mid-1990s and the small size of the domestic market. Poor infrastructure (mainly roads and communications), mountainous nature of the country and division of the country along tribal lines imposed additional costs on internal trade, thus limiting the possibilities for domestic development of manufacturing. In addition, lack of markets and non-development of a manufacturing base meant that a number of foundations of industrial economies did not develop. These include, among others, an independent commercially conversant judiciary and an enforcement system (see Chapter 3).[42]

In the 1990s, manufacturing contributed only one-third of industrial valued–added (9% of GDP). Activity was strong during 1990-1993 and declined by more than 5% in 1994.

---

[40]   Total employment in the sector is estimated by the CSO to have reached 96,673 in 2000.

[41]   About 32%, 78% and 110% for large, medium and small establishments respectively. The big differences are attributed to the low value-added of refining (a large establishment). For more details, see Al-Sabbry (2001).

[42]   Sherwood (2002).

For the whole period of 1990-1994, growth of manufacturing value added averaged only 2.1% (3.0% excluding oil refining) and was still concentrated in oil refining and production of consumer goods. The good performance during 1990-1993 was due to the fact that the sector continued to work under the umbrella of the protection system and government subsidies. The decline in output in 1994 was attributed mainly to the civil war that year which caused enormous damage to life and property. After the civil war, activity picked up and certain activities managed to grow by more than 20% (e.g., food and tobacco, cement and non-metallic products and furniture). Trade liberalization measures also contributed to the recovery as the cost of imported inputs declined and the devaluation discouraged imports of manufactured goods (Table 2.10).

TABLE 2.10: GROWTH OF MANUFACTURING SECTOR, 1990-2000 (%)

	1990-1994	1995-2000	1990-2000
Food and Tobacco	-0.6	8.2	4.6
Textiles, Clothing & Leather	5.6	-0.8	1.7
Wooden and Furniture	6.3	2.1	3.7
Paper, Printing and Publishing	6.3	1.5	3.4
Chemicals and Plastic Products	-2.0	2.8	0.9
Structural Non-metallic (Construction)	5.7	12.8	9.9
Metal Products, Machines and Equipment	8.9	1.6	4.5
Oil Refinery	-1.5	-0.5	-0.9
Total Manufacturing (including oil refining)	2.1	5.7	4.2
Manufacturing (excluding oil refining)	3.0	6.8	5.3
GDP	4.1	6.4	5.5

Source: Data from the National Accounts of the Central Statistical Office (CSO), Sana'a, 2001.

Manufacturing recovered strongly in 1995 by a growth rate of 24%, and during the period 1995-2000, it recorded an average annual growth of 5.7% (6.8% excluding oil refining) against the FFYP's planned target of 8.0% p. a. In particular, output grew by an average rate of 0.8% during 1996-1997 (1.3% excluding oil refining). A number of factors contributed to the sluggish growth during the two years. First, the impact of the civil war on Aden refinery greatly affected capacity of the refinery and output of oil refining declined by 10% in 1994, by 4% in 1996, stagnated in 1997 and declined by 7% in 1998. Second, the cost of production rose as a result of phasing out the government's implicit subsidies when tariffs for public utilities (water and electricity) were raised. Third, the stabilization program and tight growth in money and credit contributed to the slow demand for manufactured goods. Fourth, competition intensified as a result of removing all bans and quantitative restrictions on imports, elimination of import licensing, and lowering of custom tariffs. Manufacturing output started to recover in 1998 with a growth rate of 5.5% particularly in textiles, leather, chemical and plastic products. Output growth slowed in 1999 and recovered strongly in 2000 recording a 7% growth rate. Food and tobacco, cement and other non-metallic product outperformed other sub-sectors during the year. For the period 1998-2000, the sector managed to grow by an average rate of 4.3% (3.8% including refining) (Table 2.10 and Annex Table 8).

Despite expansion of the manufacturing sector in the 1990s, it is still oriented mainly to cover the domestic market and its contribution to total exports economy is still small, particularly when compared with other similar countries. While the total exports of Yemen reached 50% of GDP in 2000, manufactured exports represented less than 1% of merchandise export, 26% of non-oil merchandise exports and less than 0.5% of GDP (see

Box 4.2, Chapter 4).[43] The protectionist policies pursued until mid-1990s (subsidies, high tariffs and controlled exchange rate) were unsustainable and have contributed to the fragility and inefficiency of the sector with a great cost to the government budget and social welfare. They reserved the local markets for local production and subsidized imported raw materials and equipment. This indirectly discouraged the manufacturers from improving the quality of their products and management of their establishments. The removal of all bans on imports created a competitive market for local goods where local manufactures had to compete with imported goods, to improve their mediocre quality and to start reducing the high production costs under which they operate. After the reforms, and following a couple of years of sluggish growth, manufacturing activities started to recover in the late 1990s.

In addition to its contribution to GDP, the manufacturing sector has important fiscal contributions in the form of direct and indirect taxes (including income, production and consumption taxes as well as taxes on value-added and custom duties on imported raw material). The country's total indirect tax revenues were YR 55 billion in 1999. According to 1999 survey, the total indirect tax from the manufacturing sector was estimated at YR 10.1 billion representing about 18% of total indirect taxes. With custom duties, the contribution of manufacturing to total indirect taxes reached 21%. The large establishments contributed 98% of total indirect taxes while medium and small establishments contributed only 0.1% and 1.7% respectively.

In a survey of about 1,000 private enterprises in 2001 (see Chapter 3), manufacturing firms accounted for 23% of the sample and comprised mainly of "garment, consumer goods and other" manufacturing. The firms in the sample serve primarily the domestic market. Only 32 firms, or 3.5% of respondents are exporters. The majority of exporters are large firms and 23% are medium firms. Only size is a significant determinant of whether a firm exports confirming that larger firms are more export-oriented in Yemen. Location, age, sector and ownership type do not significantly increase the likelihood of exporting in multivariate analysis. More importantly, the survey reveals that manufacturing firms, as well as foreign-owned firms, are more likely to report violent incidents in their neighborhood. Lack of security appears to be a major constraint to manufacturing activities in Yemen.

Growth Prospects and Targets of the Second Five-Year Plan for Manufacturing

Manufacturing has been accorded a high priority by the SFYP as one of the potential engines for rapid economic growth, job creation, attraction of FDI and technical progress, and poverty reduction. The plan aims to: (i) achieve a real rate of growth of 9.2% in manufacturing output (7.5% for oil refining), which will raise the share of the sector to 9% of GDP by 2005; (ii) support the orientation towards exports, and; (iii) support and develop small-scale and traditional handicraft industries. It also hopes that the sector will make use of Yemen's comparative advantages in terms of natural resources, human resources, and the strategic location and its accessibility to major international markets. The plan also targets a big increase in exports of manufacturers, with special focus on small and medium scale industries for their ability to create job opportunities. The Plan also accords oil refining a

---

[43]   Main manufactured export goods include household cleaning products (5.1% of non-oil merchandise exports), beverage and tobacco products (4.4%) and machinery and transport equipment (7.9%).

priority and seeks to expand the refining capacities of Aden and Marib refineries and to encourage the involvement of the private sector involvement in refining.

The realization of these targets largely depends on government removal of the constraints in the sector, further trade liberalization, improving infrastructure and utilities and improving the legal and judicial systems. There are good prospects for manufacturing of food and tobacco for exports to the GCC and African countries. There are also good prospects for manufacturing of textiles, garments, construction materials, and furniture and wood work because of the comparative advantages of Yemen in such industries. Processing of agricultural products such as coffee and fish could be promoted with expansion of facilities and skills as well as improvements in quality controls and marketing facilities. The prospects of manufacturing are better with the development of the free zone in Aden.

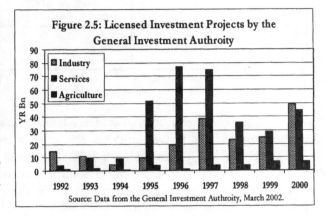

Figure 2.5: Licensed Investment Projects by the General Investment Authroity

Source: Data from the General Investment Authroity, March 2002.

Boosting manufacturing activities in Yemen would require the removal or reduction of constraints that inhibit the growth and expansion of small enterprises. The inability to identify markets, insecurity and unenforceability of contracts, inability to access land for expansion and insecurity of land tenure, lack of skills, high cost of transportation and the high cost of licenses and permits represent major constraints for business expansion (Chapter 3). Enabling manufacturers to identify and reach domestic and foreign markets through reduction of transportation cost, development of marketing facilities, business training, and improving the reliability and enforceability of contracts are critical reforms for expansion of manufacturing activities. Access to land and securing land titling is also important to attract foreign investors into the sector.[44]

Other Industrial Sub-Sectors (Construction, Water, and Electricity)

Construction value-added averaged 3.9% of GDP (12% of industrial value-added) during the last decade. Construction activity boomed in the early 1990s following the return of immigrants from the Gulf States and recorded average annual growth rate of 12.0% during 1991-1992. Construction activity slowed in 1993 and declined by 17% in 1994. Post-war recovery boosted construction to an average growth rate of 26% during 1995-1997 before decelerating to an average rate of 3.5% in the last three years. The construction and building sub-sector plays an important role in its contribution to GDP (4.2% in 2000) and its absorption of 6.6% of the total working manpower. The SFYP envisages an average annual increase in construction activities of 11% and as a result the sector's share in GDP is planned to increase from 4.2% in 2000 to 5.5% by the end of the plan.

Water and electricity (0.9% of GDP in the 1990s) grew weakly in the pre-civil war period, declined markedly in 1994 (by 14%) and recovered strongly during 1995-1996 (more

---

44 Sherwood (2002).

than 12% annual growth). The sub-sector grew by 4.0% per annum in the last four years. The relative share of this sub-sector in the GDP continued to decline in the 1990s from 1.2% in 1990 to 0.8% in 2000. It is mainly composed of the electricity and water supplies. The sub-sector performed better during the FFYP in comparison with the early 1990s (Table 2.11).

TABLE 2.11: WATER AND ELECTRICITY, VALUE-ADDED, 1990-2005

	Share of GDP (%)				Average Annual Growth Rate (%)		
	1990	1995	2000	2005 *	1990-1995	1996-2000	2001-2006 *
Electricity	0.4	0.2	0.4	..	0.2	7.4 #	..
Water	0.8	0.4	0.4	..	4.6	5.2 #	..
Total Water and Electricity	1.2	0.6	0.8	0.8	3.1	6.0	9.2

(i) * : Target, (ii) .. : Not available, and (iii) # : growth rate for the period 1995-1999.
Source: National Accounts from the Central Statistical Office (CSO), 2001 and the Second Five-Year Plan (SFYP, 2001).

The electricity sector witnessed noticeable progress over the FFYP. The installed capacity (generated power) and the sold energy increased by average annual growth rates of 5.0% and 6.4% respectively. As a result, the total electric output has reached 610 megawatt in 2000 up from 478 in 1995 and the number of subscribers increased from 524,000 to about 800,000 over the same period, which raises the number of beneficiaries from the national grid and independent systems to 5.3 million people (covering 29% of total population). In 2000, the capacity of the Public Electricity Corporation (PEC) reached 597 megawatt. Demand on the national grid was 518 megawatt and 92 megawatt on the independent systems. This resulted in a deficit of 49 megawatt in the national grid and a surplus of 36 megawatt in the independent systems. Energy losses in 2000 are estimated at 38% up from 34% in 1995. The sector suffers also from weak institutional, technical, administrative and financial systems. As will be detailed in the next chapter, electricity shortages and disruptions are identified by private sector as a major impediment to business and growth; and the sector should be accorded a higher priority by the GoY by addressing the institutional framework (reform of PEC), reduction of energy losses, liberalization of tariffs, and inviting private sector in power generation particularly by utilizing the gas resources.

In urban areas, water consumption is estimated at 376 million m³ (64% coverage for urban population). The supply of water from the public water network rose from 76 million m³ in 1995 to 103 million m³ in 2000. In rural areas, water consumption is estimated at 306 million m³ in 2000 with a coverage rate of 59% of rural population (7.7 million persons), with piped water accounting for 27% of coverage, water wells for 44% and surface water for 29%.

The SFYP aims to increase the installed capacity to 1,266 megawatt by 2005 (7.4% average annual increase) and to increase electricity coverage to 40% of total population. To achieve these targets the plan considers conversion to gas turbines and reduction of electricity losses to 33%. It considers also private sector participation in power generation and distribution. It also targets increase in rural electrification to cover 22% of rural population by 2005 (up from 16% or 2.1 million people in 2000 and 1.7 million people in 1995). Furthermore, the SFYP aims to increase supply of water for household consumption in urban areas to 163 million m³ by 2005 (9.5% average annual growth rate) to raise the average to 69%. It also targets increase in rural water consumption to 423 million m³ by 2005 (6.7% average annual increase) to raise the coverage rate to 65%.

THE SERVICES SECTOR

Yemen's services sector is dominated by government services (representing 45% of total services and 23% of GDP during 1990-2000) followed by transportation and communications (10% of GDP in 2000) and the wholesale and retail trade (7% of GDP in 2000). The cumulative contribution of other services (except real estate) to GDP growth was negligible. The real estate sector has been very dynamic and grew by an average of 5.5% in the last decade, its share in total GDP increased from 5.5% in 1990 to 6.8% by 2000, and its contribution to GDP growth has been about 7%. Other services (maintenance, social and personal services and private non-profit services) and financial institutions represented 7.3% and 4.2% of GDP respectively during 1990-2000 (see Annex Table 1). The following sections focus on tourism, transport and communications, government services and wholesale and retail trade given their current and potential impact of services value-added and GDP in general.

TABLE 2.12: SERVICES VALUE-ADDED, 1990-2005

	Share of GDP (%)				Growth Rate (%)			
			End-FFYP	Target End-SFYP	Actual	Target FFYP	Actual FFYP	Target SFYP
	1990	1995	2000	2005	1990-1995	1996-2000	1996-2000	2001-2005
1. Trade, Hotels and Restaurants & Maintenance	10.0	12.0	8.6	10.2	2.4	7.0	5.8	9.1
Wholesale and Retail Trade	8.3	9.7	7.2	8.4	2.2	..	5.9	9.0
Hotels and Restaurants	0.7	1.0	0.7	0.9	2.3	..	7.9	10.7
Maintenance and Repairs	0.9	1.2	0.8	0.9	3.8	..	3.7	8.3
2. Transportation, Communication & Storage	15.5	12.6	10.3	12.2	-4.8	10.0	2.2	9.1
3. Finance, Insurance and Real Estate	9.8	9.6	7.8	9.3	2.0	8.0	6.3	9.5
Finance and Insurance	3.7	3.7	2.9	3.8	-2.1	..	6.6	12.0
Real Estate and Business Services	6.1	5.9	4.9	5.5	3.9	..	6.2	8.0
4. Personal and Social Services	1.1	1.2	0.8	0.9	2.2	8.0	6.7	6.5
5. Government Services	16.9	12.9	10.8	10.4	13.0	10.0	5.7	4.7
6. NGOs	0.1	0.1	0.1	0.1	-0.7	..	14.9	5.0
TOTAL SERVICES VALUE ADDED	47.9	48.3	38.5	43.1	4.8	8.7	5.3	8.0

Sources: National accounts data for 1990-2000 from the Central Statistical Organization (CSO), and the Second Five-Year Plan (SFYP; 2001) for 2001-2005.

Tourism

The contribution of tourism to GDP and economic growth in Yemen has been insignificant. The actual contribution of tourism may have been slightly underestimated in the national accounts because the impact of the sector is measured by the contribution of hotels and restaurants only. It accounted for only 0.5% of GDP in the 1990s and its growth averaged 5.3% during the decade. Following the drop in the value-added of the sub-sector in 1994 by 12%, value added of hotels and restaurants increased by an average of 9% during 1995-2000. Nonetheless, the contribution of the sub-sector into GDP growth remained negligible. The SFYP considers the tourism sector as one of the leading and promising sectors for its ability to provide job opportunities, poverty reduction and foreign currencies given Yemen's potential in cultural, historical, environmental aestivation, coastal and island tourism in addition to mountain climbing and desert scouting. The Strategic Vision 2025 hopes to increase the number of tourists in Yemen from 73,000 in 2000 to 2 million visitors by the end of the Plan.

Recent Trends and the Present Situation

With an estimated GDP contribution of 1.7% (hotels and restaurants contribute only 0.7% to GDP), tourism in Yemen represents a marginal economic sector. Gross receipts generated by tourism are estimated at about RY 23 billion or US$ 135 million in 2000.[45] About 56% of the revenues are contributed by international tourists whose arrivals in 2000 totaled 72,836 (35% from the Middle East, 34% from Europe, 11% from Asia, 11% from the Americas, and 8% from Africa). With an average length of stay of 6.5 days and an average daily expenditure of US$ 160, these arrivals generated total gross foreign exchange revenues of US$ 76 million (see Annex Table 4-7).[46] International vacation tourism was well below potential and is estimated at 25% of the tourist arrivals (18,000 visitors) mainly culture and adventure tourism. The 5 and 4 stars hotels that account for 32% of total room capacity mainly caters for international tourism traffic.

TABLE 2.13: VALUE ADDED AND EMPLOYMENT BY HOTELS AND RESTAURANTS, 1999

Size of establishment	Value added (YR '000)	Number of employees
Large	1,115,490	353,397
Medium and Small	18,885,552	3,932,344
Total	**20,000,042**	**4,285,741**

Source: Data from the 1999 Services Survey, the Central Statistical Office (CSO), 2001.

After growing by some 35% from 1995 to 1998, tourist arrivals registered a sharp decline in 1999 (due to the negative impact of Abyan kidnapping) followed by a partial recovery in 2000 (Figure 2.6). Hotel capacity for international traffic (i.e., 5 and 4 stars) expanded from 1,072 to 2,589 rooms or 140% from 1995 to 2000 in anticipation of increased business and vacation traffic despite the fact that most hotels experienced unsustainably low annual occupancy rates (estimated at 30% over the last three years).[47]

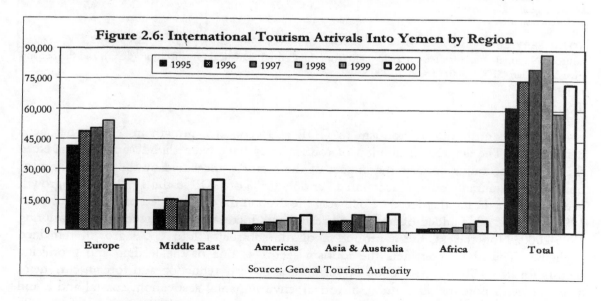

Figure 2.6: International Tourism Arrivals Into Yemen by Region

Source: General Tourism Authority

---

[45] Including all expenditures, notably accommodation, food, transportation and purchases, Brrizi (2001) estimate the contribution of international tourism to GDP in 2000 at RY 13 billion or US$ 76 million.

[46] The estimate can decline to US$ 61 million if daily spending average is estimated at US$ 130.

[47] Brizzi (2001) estimates that total revenues of these hotels about RY8 billion or US$ 48 million.

Domestic tourism contributes 44% to total tourism receipts. It is mainly business oriented and small in size because of the absence of a vibrant modern economy. Domestic recreational and cultural tourism is insignificant because of social and behavioral factors as well as income constraints.[48] Domestic tourism consists of business traffic which is in itself very limited and mainly related to visiting purposes rather than conventions, training or other business-related activities. Presently, expatriates living in Yemen are the main contributors to domestic tourism. The overall contribution of domestic tourism to GDP in 2000 is estimated at RY 10 billion or US$ 59 million.

Constraints and Challenges to Development of Tourism in Yemen

Tourism in Yemen, and international vacation tourism in particular, faces many constraints, the most notable are (i) poor and expensive transportation; (ii) difficult operating environment for tourism, (iii) weak promotion, (iv) lack of promotion activities, (v) insecurity, and (vi) the challenges of preserving cultural heritage. Tapping the identified potentials in the sector, therefore, requires concerted efforts by the authorities to remove these constraints.

Air accessibility to Yemen is limited and international and domestic airfares are high compared to other tourism destinations. Although Yemen's international vacation tourism clientele may be less price sensitive, because it comprises mainly relatively rich cultural and adventure tourists rather than mass tourists, its expansion requires a reassessment of present air policies. Internal air travel for international tourists is hampered by high fares, air schedules that do not fit tourist circuit needs, frequent flight delays and cancellations. Authorities should also look at ways to facilitate air access by foreign airlines and reduce air access costs. This may require liberalizing landing rights, reviewing landing fees, allowing charter flights, and opening to international traffic additional airports. Although entry visa requirements have been eased, their cost is still high. More importantly tourists who exit Yemen for visiting neighboring countries have to renew and pay for an additional visa at re-entry, a requirement that hampers the development of regional circuit tourism.

Public resources for tourism promotion are limited. These resources should be spent effectively on activities targeting the most promising demand segments and that can leverage private funding. Relevant ministries and agencies should develop coordinated strategies to use their available resources consonantly to the above objective. Considerable progress has been achieved recently in promoting tourism through exhibitions of Yemen's cultural heritage and archeological treasures. This could be expanded and be combined with well-targeted and effective tourism promotion campaigns by the specialized media and press.

Investment into tourism is negatively affected by most of the constraints that hamper business development in Yemen (see Chapter 3). Private investors interested in the development of tourism facilities find a difficult, if not hostile, investment environment. They cannot invest unless they associate with local partners who often have no financial capacity. Access to land, permit demands, connections to utilities often require lengthy procedures, murky processes and costly transactions. Even the choice of contractors and

---

[48]   For estimates of tourism revenues, contribution to GDP, and estimates of international and domestic tourism, see Brizzi (2001).

suppliers for the development of tourist facilities could be complicated by the demands of local officials and tribesmen in many locations. Furthermore, operating tourism facilities and services is as difficult as developing them. Owners and managers are often asked to provide free services and special favors; often subject to frequent harassment by customs and tax officials, and there are often requests of protection money. The weak judicial system and the public administration aggravate the situation. Lack of trained personnel has been cited as an important constraint by investors.

Yemen has experienced numerous cases of kidnapping. Though most of these ended without major consequences for the individuals concerned, the impact of kidnappings on vacation tourism has been severer. This can be measured by the scope of hotel cancellations following the announcement of a kidnapping. Based on the information provided by the largest tour operators, in some instances, these reached 60% of the acquired reservations.

Vacation tourists visit Yemen because of its pristine landscape of mountains, valleys uncontaminated by the signs of modern civilization and the beauty of its cities and villages whose harmonious urban fabric and architecture remains unspoiled from spurious urban development patterns, building types and material. Protecting the natural environment and cultural heritage of Yemen is a prerequisite for maintaining and enhancing vacation tourism arrivals. This calls for the establishment of effective environmental protection and cultural heritage preservation policies and laws and, more important, for ensuring that the agencies responsible for their enforcement,[49] develop the necessary managerial and technical capability. Another challenge is preserving the traditional life of the dwellers of cities and villages while improving their living standards and their access to infrastructure services. This calls for the development of awareness on the values of traditional architecture, handicraft activities, and life styles among local government officials, local community organizations, and local civil society.

Growth Prospects of Tourism Activities

It is difficult to predict tourism growth in Yemen, particularly in the more distant future. Overall, international business traffic is projected to increase over the next five years by just slightly above GDP growth rates. In the long-run, business tourism is projected to grow at an accelerated pace as the modern sectors of the economy expand and Aden and other coastal cities establish themselves as major industrial and commercial centers. The activities generated by trade, oil industry, international relations, and development assistance are expected to remain major contributors to future growth, with the service and manufacturing industries gradually completing the picture.

Conversely, vacation tourism could possibly increase by up to three folds if the constraints in the sector are removed. Existing and under construction room capacity for international tourism should be able to accommodate much of such increase. The number of international arrivals for cultural and eco-tourism is well below potential. Even though the total demand associated to these segments represents a limited share of the broad

---

[49] These include the Environmental Protection Authority (EPA), the General Organization for the Protection of Cultural Heritage in Yemen (GOPHCY) and the General Organization for Antiquities, Manuscripts and Museums (GOAMM).

international vacation market and therefore cannot count on a large number of potential clients, it is expanding worldwide and Yemen is well positioned to capture a much larger portion of it. Offering visitors a stay that can combine cultural and eco-tourism with beach tourism can facilitate such expansion. Yemen could also look at the possibility of being part of regional circuits combining its cultural and eco-tourism product with recreational or beach based tourism in the UAE, Oman and Djibouti. Tapping the vacation tourism potentials would, nonetheless, require the development of new capacity in selected destinations, including the creation of resort complexes at beach locations. Expectations for beach resort tourism development should be however realistic. It is unlikely that Yemen will be able to become a mass tourism destination. This will require competing with countries that are endowed with better assets and have already developed capacity and image. Scuba diving in Socotra and the Red Sea Islands also presents some potential but it is bound to be a niche market within the broader scuba diving market.

A big segment of the international vacation tourism market is represented by visitors from the Gulf countries and Yemeni nationals living abroad. This market is very diversified and includes a variety of tourism motivations such as recreational facilities in specialized destinations (e.g., Aden, Yemen highlands, religious and therapeutic sites). Though there is no reliable information on this market, it appears that it is developing and presents considerable scope for growth. To tap it, it is however essential that Yemeni or foreign investors develop appropriate accommodation facilities, such as villa complexes, in resort areas endowed with recreational amenities.

The same expectations apply to domestic tourism. At least in the short-run, the growth pace of business tourism is likely to be the same as, or slightly exceed, GDP growth because of the progressive modernization of the economy. Recreational tourism would grow faster as it starts from a very low base and gradually develops into an established activity while the country urbanizes, personal income increases and social behaviors evolve. Again, existing capacity should be able to absorb the bulk of additional demand, though the development of recreational tourism calls for the establishment of appropriate accommodation and other tourism facilities in selected destinations. Coastal areas in the vicinity of Aden, Zabid and Mukalla as well as resort villages in the vicinity of Sana'a, Taiz and Seyoun appear to be the most likely candidates to attract this demand.

Consonant with the above expectations and provided that the international political and economic situation is stable and Yemen's economy grows at 5.6% on average during the next five years as foreseen by the SFYP, total tourism receipts could grow to reach some RY 37.5 billion or US$ 215 million by 2005.[50] If this were to materialize, the contribution of the tourism sector to GDP would slightly increase from 1.7% in 2000 to 2.1% in 2005.

---

[50] Gianni (2001) projects that a reasonable objective for Yemen will be to triple within the next 5 years its present vacation tourism arrivals. As a result we can at best expect that, overall, international arrivals will grow from 73,000 in 2000 (with 18,000 vacation arrivals) to 127,000 in 2005 (with 54,000 vacation arrivals). Within this framework, international tourist receipts, could possibly increase from RY 13 billion or US$ 76 million in 2000 to over RY 23 billion or US$ 135 million in 2005. He also projects that it is unlikely that domestic vacation tourism can contribute more than 20% to the expansion of the overall domestic tourism during the next five years. As the result of the above assumptions, domestic tourism could grow from some RY 10 billion or US$ 59 million in 2000 to YR 14 billion or US$ 80 million in 2005.

Government Services

The services sector in Yemen is dominated by government services (administration) representing 45% of total services and 23% of GDP during 1990-2000. Not only government administration and services contributed about a quarter of GDP, they were very dynamic and contributed about half of GDP growth. Government services increased by an average of 15.3% during 1991-1995 before decelerating to an average of 5.6% during the second half

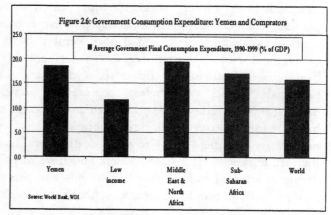

Figure 2.6: Government Consumption Expenditure: Yemen and Comprators

Average Government Final Consumption Expenditure, 1990-1999 (% of GDP)

Yemen Low income Middle East & North Africa Sub-Saharan Africa World

Source: World Bank, WDI

of the 1990s. Given the present large size of government in the economy (Figure 2.7) in comparison with other countries, this sector will continue to play an important role in economic development and growth.

During 2001-2005, government services are planned to increase by an annul average of 4.7% and their share in GDP will therefore decline slightly from 10.8% in 2000 to 10.4% by 2005. The priorities of the SFYP can be judged by the projected allocations of government spending. Spending on defense and law and order and spending on mining and oil are planned to receive the same share of total government spending (25% and 7%, respectively). Social services share will increase from 34% to 37%; the share of agriculture and fisheries will increase from 2.4% to 2.8%, while government spending on transport and communications is expected to decline from 0.4% to 0.3%.

Transportation and Communications

Transport and storage represent one-fifth of services value-added. Their share in GDP growth, however, continued to decline from about 15% in 1990 to 10% in 2000, and their contribution to GDP growth has been negative. The sub-sector recorded negative growth rates throughout 1993-1996 and only recovered in 1997-2000. Therefore, the performance of the sub-sector was disappointing during the FFYP when the sector grew by an annual average of 2.2% against a target of 10%. Despite liberalization and deregulation efforts, the whole sector remained largely under control of state monopolies such as Yemen Navigation Line, Land Transport Company and Yemenia. The government also controls most of the tariffs and fares.

Road transportation is by far the most important transport sub-sector with the number of registered vehicles in Yemen reaching 885,000 in 2000. The sector was liberalized in the 1990s and private sector participation has increased in road transport. Licenses were issued by the General Land Transport Authority (established in 1999) for private sector transport offices to enhance competition and reduce transport cost, in addition to issuance of licenses to private companies for mass transportation of passengers between cities and in tourism. The roads network, however, is still very weak despite expansion during the FFYP. Paved roads do not exceed 9% of total roads (11 km for every 1,000 km²). The trucking sector is still controlled by the private (Ferzah) cartel, which fixes prices and prevents entry thus raising transportation costs.[51] More important, even in areas with available road networks, overland security is often limited by security concerns.

TABLE 2.14: ROAD TRANSPORT NETWORK IN YEMEN

	1995	2000	Target 2005
Asphalt roads (km)	5,052	6,586	10,947
Gravel roads (km)	2,360	3,915	6,109
Rural dirt roads (km)	..	60,000	..

Source: Computed from data contained in the SFYP. (..) : Not available.

Yemen has an advantageous position in the international shipping network and many regional and international shipping lines pass through its ports, especially Aden and Hodeidah. Consequently, the marine transport and seaport sector plays an important role in economic activity in Yemen and 68% of Yemen's non–oil exports and approximately 85% of the country's imports leave and enter through seaports, in addition to shipping services (e.g., agencies, cargo handling, forwarding) and ship maintenance and repairs. During the FFYP, marine transport witnessed significant expansion. In 1997, a new dock was constructed in Al-Salif seaport. A container seaport was constructed in Aden and an armlet was constructed in the island of Socotra. Work is currently underway for the construction of three new seaports in Hadhramout, Al-Mahra, and Abyan. The number of ships calling on Yemen's six ports increased from 2,407 in 1995 to 3,409 in 2000. The cargo handled also rose from about 4.2 million tons to 6.4 million over the same period. During the FFYP, private sector involvement in marine transportation and services increased particularly in handling cargo, supplying ships, and concessions to operate the new container port in Aden.

Yemen has 14 airports, 6 of which are international. During the FFYP, many airports and facilities have been constructed or rehabilitated including Aden, Ataq, Taiz, Al-Rayyan and Al-Ghaeidha and Socotra Airports. Airline fleet was also upgraded. Air traffic, however, declined significantly over the last few years. The number of incoming and departing passengers declined to 1.1 million passengers in 2000 down from about 1.4 million passengers in 1995. Air-cargo, nonetheless, rose from 9,300 tons to 12,800 tons over the same period. The decline in air traffic led to the withdrawal of some international carriers, thus reducing the number of such carriers to 12 companies out of 38 companies that signed bilateral agreements with Yemen. Yemenia's (the national air carrier) share of the airline passengers reached 66% of total passenger traffic through the Yemeni airports in 2000 and 56% of the air cargo traffic. The decline in air traffic was caused partly by the decline in tourist arrivals into Yemen.

The communications and postal services sub-sector in Yemen is shared by the public, mixed and private sectors. It witnessed significant expansion during the FFYP in addition to receiving increased government investments well in excess of what was targeted during the FFYP (Box 2.3). Fiber-optic connections between major cities, digital telephone exchange networks, introduction of mobile telephones and the internet services were the major achievements during the FFYP. Telephone capacity increased from 242,499 lines in 1995 to 460,736 in 2000. The installed lines almost doubled from 183,348 lines to 346,709 over the same period and accordingly telephone coverage in Yemen is now 2 telephone lines for every 100 persons. Similarly, the postal services also witnessed significant growth during

---

[51]   IMF (2001; 76).

the FFYP (reaching 42,229 post office boxes in 2000 from 8,120 boxes in 1995). About 59 postal service offices were established in a number of governorates, and the overland mail transport network was enhanced. The postal agency contracts now cover many rural remote areas. The express-mail and courier service companies were also active over the last few years and 7 companies were licensed to operate in Yemen.

BOX 2.3: TELECOMMUNICATIONS MARKET IN YEMEN

A Republican Decree was issued in 1991 creating the Public Telecommunication Corporation (PTC), a 100% government-owned corporation. It is the product of a merger between the North Yemen's Public Telecom Corporation (PTC) and South Yemen's YemenTel, the two entities that, prior to unification, were in charge of telecommunications. The Ministry of Communications is considered a regulatory and supervisory agency for the entire telecommunications sector and its Minister is the Chairman of the PTC board.

PTC has the exclusive right to provide fixed domestic telecommunication services. The right to provide international services has been granted to TeleYemen on a monopoly basis until 2003. Internet services have been provided also by TeleYemen, but not under any agreement and, therefore, PTC has recently established its own internet service (The Yemen Internet Gateway). Mobile (cellular) services have been liberalized in 2000 and two private companies (Sabafon and Spacetel) now provide GSM mobile services. Hundreds of telecommunication centers were established throughout the country where phones are put at the disposal of the public and users pay cash once their calls are completed. The Ministry of Communications issues permission for these centers and the PTC provides the service. In addition, pay phones were also set up on the streets throughout the country by a private company (Yemen Payphone Company Ltd). Wake-up calls, conference calls and paging are also offered but coverage is very low.

TeleYemen, a joint venture between Cable & Wireless and PTC, was established by a cabinet decree in 1990. Under the terms of a 10-year agreement between Cable & Wireless and the Government, the Cable & Wireless was to acquire, at first, 65% of the capital of TeleYemen, while PTC acquired 35%. The share of the two companies were to change to 51% for Cable & Wireless and 49% for PTC after 3 years and to change again to 35% for Cable & Wireless and 65% for PTC in 1995. However, the government decided to limit its participation to 49%. The Board consists of 8 members, 4 representing Cable & Wireless and the other 4 representing PTC and the Chairman of the Board is the Minister of Communications. The agreement is valid until December 2003 and negotiations for its renewal will start in October 2002.

TeleYemen had been first entrusted in 1990 to provide international calls, telegram, and telex services. In 1992, the government authorized TeleYemen to set up mobile services and later in 1996 it authorized it to offer internet services. While Internet and international services were still monopolized by TeleYemen, the GSM mobile services were liberalized in 2000; . Two private companies: Sabafon (a venture of Egypt's Orascom) and Spacetel (joint venture between Lebanon's Investcom and Oman's Al-Zubeir Group) currently provide GSM services. Sabafon subscribers reached 100,000 in 2002.

All regulatory powers are concentrated in the hands of the Minister of Communications, who is also Chairman of PTC and TeleYemen. Telecommunication prices are usually studied and proposed by a committee composed of members of PTC and the Ministry. Then the Cabinet has the right to issue decisions on prices. For international communications, the agreement between Cable and Wireless and the Government provides for adjustments aimed at maintaining price-equivalent in hard currency. The Cabinet again approves these adjustments.

Source: PTC Yemen, April 2002

The GoY seeks to complete and update the domestic and international road networks during the SFYP to link all governorates with each other and to link Yemen with its neighboring countries. In addition to the new roads to be constructed (Table 2.14) the plan also aims to maintain about 5,000 km of asphalt roads and 2,500 km of gravel roads, to introduce local and foreign investors in the construction and operation of roads through BOT and BOO mechanisms, to strengthen road safety measures. Secondly, the SFYP aims to reduce the cost of marine transport and freight shipping by uplifting the capacities and capabilities of the seaports and upgrading the efficiency of their operations, and to introduce regular domestic marine transport within Yemeni seaports and with other regional and international seaports. Thirdly, the plan also targets doubling of telephone connections (1 million subscribers) so that the coverage will reach 4 telephone lines for every 100 persons (16.7% growth per annum), restructuring tariffs for services, increasing capacity of mobile phones by adding 400,000 new subscribers and extending the coverage to rural areas, expanding postal network by setting up 168 post office and granting addition postal agencies. Evidence now suggests that open competition in telecom markets, with no exclusivity for new entrants, is the fastest way to improve telecom access.

Wholesale and Retail Trade

The trade sub-sector grew by an average of 4.3% in the 1990s and its contribution to GDP growth has been relatively weak. Trade activities declined by 13% in 1994 due to the civil war and picked up in 1995 at 15.5% mainly due to import and excise tax reforms. It recorded an average annul growth rate of 6.0% during 1996-2000, boosted by trade liberalization policies adopted since mid-1990s. The growth rate of wholesale and retail trade increased from 2.2% during 1990-1995 to 5.9% during the FFYP. The number of manpower involved in trade activities increased from 295,000 in 1992 to 407,000 in 2000 (11% of total labor force).

While the impact of external trade on economic growth and development is well documented from the experience of other countries, domestic trade can also play an important role in job creation and income generation in addition to its impact on other economic sectors and activities (e.g., agriculture and manufacturing). The SFYP aims to increase the share of trade in GDP (by one percentage point of GDP by 2005).

PART II:

PRIVATE SECTOR ENVIRONMENT
AND GOVERNANCE

CHAPTER 3:
DEVELOPING THE PRIVATE SECTOR AND IMPROVING GOVERNANCE

OVERVIEW AND MAJOR FINDINGS

The most sustainable way to alleviate poverty in Yemen is through the dynamic creation of large numbers of well-paid jobs in the private sector. Over the last three decades, the experience of most other successful small countries has shown that poverty is best reduced through a combination of rising private sector employment, increased labor productivity and higher real wages. Market-based growth, encouraging firms and workers to invest in physical equipment as well as human capital (skills), has been demonstrated as the path to better living standards for all.[52] There is substantial evidence demonstrating the need for improving total factor productivity in the Yemeni economy as an important source of growth (Chapter 1). One of the primary drivers of productivity improvement and strong growth performance is the capability of firms, which is greatest when operating in a healthy investment climate. Well-functioning private markets are also a powerful way to help the poor catch-up by providing the opportunity to enhance living standards.

Both the Strategic Vision 2025 and the SFYP recognize the pivotal role of the private sector in achieving a high and sustained rate of economic growth. They call for strengthening of the partnership between private and public sectors while according the private sector the leading role in realizing economic and social development. The SFYP aims to raise the share of the private sector in total GDP, and in non-oil GDP to 53.7% and 72.3% respectively by 2005. This would require a real growth in private sector value-added by an average annual rate of 10%. The plan also recognizes the importance of legislative and institutional reforms, reinforcing competition and improved financial intermediation to ensure efficiency in the use of resources and creation of a conducive environment for private activity. The state's role will be confined to ensuring a stable macroeconomic environment (e.g., low inflation and flexible exchange rate regime) and provision of sovereign functions and some limited economic activities and social services. The plan contains an ambitious privatization program and sees a role for the private sector in the provision of infrastructure.[53]

This chapter assesses the current status in the development of the Yemeni private sector, its contribution to economic growth and highlights the major impediments in the current business environment. It also points to a set of approaches that can be adopted by Yemen to achieve a more dynamic and job-creating private sector. In addition to available literature and studies, the analysis in this chapter relies mainly on the results of the private sector survey, which was undertaken in November 2001 specifically for the purpose of this study. The size of the sample was 947 private enterprises in 5 governorates in Yemen.

---

[52] See, for example, World Bank (1995). While quality of human capital is an important ingredient for firm productivity, it is not covered in details in this Report.
[53] The privatization program under the plan seeks to prepare 61 PEs for privatization. These include 5 PEs in the transport sector, 13 in manufacturing, 15 in agriculture, 8 in trade, 17 in fisheries in addition to the oil refinery and two public banks [See SFYP(2001)].

The main findings of this chapter include the following: (i) private sector firms in Yemen are languishing in an environment characterized by weak governance and corruption, regulatory arbitrariness, high taxes and inefficient tax administration and unfair business practices; (ii) the majority of firms are small, service oriented workshops operating in captured domestic markets with few opportunities for profitable expansion; (iii) the investment climate is viewed as a high-risk and characterized by lack of a level playing field for foreign and domestic firms; (iv) small firms face relatively minimal difficulties in entering a market, but face significant obstacles to growth in value-added and specialization as a result of high levels of risk and uncertainty in the general investment climate, unfair competition, administrative obstacles created by the lack of coordination among government departments, costly and uncompetitive infrastructure services; (v) access to electricity, land and legal services is difficult and costly, together with high transactions costs associated with incidences of crime, theft, insufficient internal transport networks and others; and, (vi) larger firms tend to do better because they are able to internalize the risks, in part through conglomeration and building up in-house capacity in critical inputs. Larger firms also tend to benefit from well-entrenched networks of influence, access to external markets and finance.

The main challenge for Yemen is then how to attain a dynamic and broad-based growth in the private sector, given its three critical and inter-related factors: (i) the weak institutional environment for the private sector in terms of weak governance and few market-promoting institutions; (ii) weak infrastructure; and, (iii) the small size of the manufacturing sector, and the persistently small size of most Yemeni firms. Policy recommendations in this chapter focus on systemic approaches to issues but also fast track methods for addressing critical bottlenecks (enclaves or industrial zones) while providing important demonstration effects in the short run. Priorities for action explored in this chapter include promoting macroeconomic stability and legal certainty, minimizing administrative regulations, addressing corruption and unfair business practices (e.g., corruption), and improving the quality of infrastructure services.

Improving the investment climate will require greater attention to improving the functioning of markets and infrastructure networks. There are three required building blocks in this approach. First, there is a need to strengthen commitment to building an economy based on market disciplines and income incentives through prudent macroeconomic management, open trade policies and a competitive exchange rate. Over the medium term, the diversification from oil will require policies to create a competitive industrial sector. Second, priorities for action also include developing formal, market-based institutions including a framework of commercial law and a workable legal system, which supports market-based transactions. Strengthening of public sector capacity in facilitating business entry and growth and tax administration is also an important component of developing effective agencies and institutions to support the development of a market economy. Third, ensuring competitive access to infrastructure such as electricity, land, water and telecommunications as well as fair competition in product markets is crucial for enhancing the profitable expansion of firms.

CHARACTERISTICS OF THE PRIVATE SECTOR AND THE INVESTMENT CLIMATE

Yemen's private sector is small and its relative importance to GDP continued to decline in the late 1990s. Despite difficulties in obtaining accurate data on its size and contribution to GDP, available estimates show that the share of private sector value-added in total GDP was about 66% of GDP in 1995, but continued to decline during the FFYP. Private sector value-added declined to 58% during 1996-1997, rising to 66% in 1998 (reflecting collapse in oil prices) before starting its decline to 55% in 1999 and further to 44% in 2000. Private sector output as a ratio of non-oil GDP, increased from 77% in 1995 to 80% in 1997 and remained at about 78% during 1998-1999 before declining to 66% in 2000 (Table 3.1).

TABLE 3.1: GDP BY PRIVATE/PUBLIC SECTOR, 1995-2005

	1995	2000		Target 2005		
	Ratio to GDP (%)	MN YR at 2000 prices	Ratio to GDP (%)	MN YR at 2000 prices	Ratio to GDP (%)	Average Annual Growth Rate, (%), 2001-2005
Non-Oil Sector	86.5	914,343	66.3	1,346,500	74.3	8.0
Oil Sector	13.5	465,469	33.7	465,500	25.7	0.0
Private Sector	66.2	605,131	43.9	973,132	53.7	10.0
Public Sector (incl. Oil)	33.8	774,681	56.1	838,868	46.3	1.6
Total GDP	**100.0**	**1,379,812**	**100.0**	**1,812,000**	**100.0**	**5.6**

Source: Second Five-Year Plan (SFYP, 2001) and data from the Central Statistical Organization (CSO).

Private investment (mainly domestic) also witnessed sharp increase during 1995-1997 and a sharp decline in 1998-1999 before modest recovery in 2000. This can bee seen also from the trend of new investment projects licensed by the GIA during 1992-2000 (Figure 3.1). Private foreign investment projects licensed by the GIA remained at about YR 6 billion during 1995-1999 and jumped to YR 22 billion in 2000.

FIGURE 3.1: INVESTMENT PROJECTS LICENSED BY THE GENERAL INVESTMENT AUTHORITY BY NATIONALITY, 1992-2000
(YR billions)

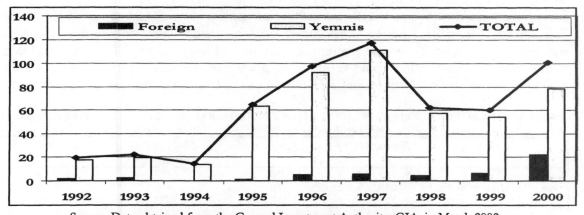

Source: Data obtained from the General Investment Authority, GIA, in March 2002.

The small size of the contribution of private sector in the economy as well as the rapid fluctuations in its contribution are partly attributed to the dominance of the oil sector in the economy in the 1990s. The oil sector dominates Yemen's exports, with a relatively small direct impact on employment and wages. As of 2000, Yemen was the 90th largest exporter in the world, with US$ 3.7 billion a year in exports, with non-oil exports contributing a mere US$ 0.4 billion. Given the more capital-intensive and niche nature of the oil industry, such an industrial structure leaves relatively little scope for private sector job creation, and can contribute to uncertainties about fiscal policy. Although there is no evidence of a "Dutch Disease" problem in Yemen (chapter 2)[54], with Yemen's relatively less-developed financial sector, there would also likely be an inefficient investment of resources by private sector beneficiaries of the oil revenue (Box 3.1).

BOX 3.1: PUBLIC AND PRIVATE SECTOR CONSEQUENCES OF AN OIL BOOM

In many developing countries, dependence on mineral exports has been associated with boom-bust cycles in fiscal spending and volatility in the macro environment, a crowding out of the private sector and higher cost structures for private sector firms. The fiscal revenues from oil and gas production fuel wide-scale public sector employment increases and high levels of investment in infrastructure. Following an oil price decline, governments tend to cancel investment projects rather than lay off public workers, leading to a climate of uncertainty for private sector firms.

In addition, as a result of unfavorable movements in the real exchange rate associated with the Dutch Disease, non-oil productive activities tend to disappear and the private sector is generally reduced to the construction sector and a number of service industries that rely heavily on government development projects. Both the expansion of public employment and the shrinkage in private sector activities tend to make the economy more vulnerable to oil price fluctuations. Studies of resource booms in many countries have shown that, besides the Dutch Disease problem, poorly developed private sector institutions can cause adverse consequences to efficient production and growth in the presence of oil booms.

Simply put, in the absence of good economic information, oil gains that flow to private sector agents can prompt myopic responses from them. This can have serious consequences if the economy does not have developed financial markets. A deficient financial market does not provide sufficient instruments to attract savings from those who gain from the windfall, leading to a sub-optimal allocation of resources in the economy (mostly over-investment in boom-related sectors, about which the beneficiaries of the resources have more information).

Sources: Devlin (2001) and Gelb (1988).

Increasing the size and scope of the non-oil private sector is Yemen's primary challenge in terms of job-creation. Excluding oil, gas and refining, the industrial sector contributed less than 10% of GDP in 2000. Within this, the non-oil manufacturing sector was less than 5% of GDP in 2000 (down from 12.6% of GDP in 1995). The private service sector comprised 44% of GDP in 2000, but almost two-thirds of the sector was concentrated in trade, tourism and transportation, traditionally not sources of high productivity or wages. Given the higher productivity and wages in manufacturing (and thus better living standards that could result from more productive manufacturing jobs), the troubling statistic is that manufacturing employed only 2.5% of Yemen's work force in 2000.

TABLE 3.2: INVESTMENT PROJECTS LICENSED BY THE GENERAL INVESTMENT AUTHORITY (GIA)
(Millions of Yemeni Rials during March 1992 to September 2002)

Sector	Yemenis	Arab	Non-Arab Foreigners	Total
Industrial	213,799	7,753	8,957	230,509
Agricultural Exc. Fisheries	23,558	580	-	24,139
Fisheries	10,185	510	1,712	12,406
Services exc. Tourism	216,823	16,474	17,145	250,423
Tourism	95,063	1,501	744	97,309
TOTAL	559,428	26,819	28,559	614,806

Source: Data obtained from the General Investment Authority, March 2002.

The size of most private firms in Yemen is small, and remuneration in these small firms is low—and growth both in size and compensation is slow. This suggests the presence

---

[54] The phenomenon is named after the 1960s crisis in the Dutch manufacturing sector caused by the export boom in natural gas. The oil windfall, by generating an increase in export earnings, increases demand for non-traded goods and, because of higher non-tradable prices and wages, lowers the competitiveness of traded goods

of substantial barriers to the growth of smaller firms. The Industrial Survey of 1999 showed that only 288 firms (less than 1% of manufacturing firms) had more than 10 employees. About 95% of firms had three or fewer employees and these numbers were virtually unchanged from 1996. Much of private manufacturing in Yemen is by one- and two-person firms, producing small amounts of the product, distributing/selling directly to customers, with little interaction with intermediaries. The resulting inability to achieve any economies of scale or scope, and the lack of specialization of skills, means that while new entry into the sector is always possible, most existing firms are not growing larger and more efficient. And compensation in these mostly smaller firms was over 50% lower than in larger firms.

Smallness is not a function of age, as the average age of firms is 14.2 years, based on a recent survey of 947 firms in 5 governorates (Box 3.2). In addition to being small, the majority of firms have concentrated ownership (single proprietorship) and are engaged in simple, low value-added activities: shop keeping, hairdressing, plumbing, together with carpentry shops, car repair and welding workshops. Most firms are structured as limited partnerships and proprietorships with 12% of large companies being public shareholding firms, while 28% are government owned. Level of foreign ownership among firms is very low and most firms are directed towards production for the domestic market (see Annex Tables 11 and 12).

BOX 3.2: YEMEN PRIVATE SECTOR ENVIRONMENT SURVEY 2001

The survey of 947 firms, randomly selected within each of 5 governorates in Yemen, was carried out in November 2001. The table below summarizes the sample characteristics. The classifications for size follow the Yemen Industrial Survey, with small firms defined as 3 or less total employees, medium (4–9 total employees) and large (10 or more total employees). The classification in itself indicates the general lack of scale in the private sector: in other countries the definition for large firms is usually 100 plus employees. Only 30 firms in the sample have over 50 total employees, and only 11 report over 100 total workers. The median number of employees is 2, but in reflection of the small number of very large firms the average is 10.5. The majority of large firms (68%) are located in Sana'a, where the average number of total workers is 25.3. Large firms tend to have marginally more experience (mean is 15.7 years), although the difference in average age is not statistically significant. The sample average age of firms is 14.2 years, and the median age is 10 years.

Location	No.	Valid (%)	Size (Total Emp.)	No.	Valid (%)	Age	No.	Valid (%)
Sana'a	265	27.98	Small (< 3 Employees)	568	66.75	Est. 1991 & earlier	450	51.31
Aden	249	26.29	Medium (4-9 Employees)	165	19.39	Est. 1992-1998	264	30.10
Taiz	200	21.12	Large (> 10 Employees)	118	13.87	Est. 1999-2000	163	18.59
Hodeidah	106	11.19						
Hadramout	127	13.41	No Response/Can's Say	96		No Response/Can't Say	70	
Total	**947**	**100.00**	**Total**	**947**	**100.00**	**Total**	**947**	**100.00**

Single proprietorship is by far the most common legal organization for firms (83.5%), followed by partnership (10.7%). Only 4.4% of respondents are incorporated. Partnerships and corporations are more likely as firm size increases. The majority (66%) of corporations are located in Sana'a, with 12% in Aden, 7% Taiz and the remaining 15% in Hodeidah.

The majority (60.4%) of the firms in the sample operate in the services sector, largely in the trade (29.3%) and 'other services' (22.3%) categories. Manufacturing firms account for 22.6% of the sample, comprised mainly of 'other manufacturing' (11.6%), garments (4.4%) and consumer goods (3.6%). Construction (2.2%), electricity gas and water (1.2%), and agriculture (1.2%) are the largest sub-sectors defined within the 'other sector' category. The firms in the sample are almost entirely privately owned. Only 10 firms, or 1.4% of respondents reported any government ownership.

Small and medium sized enterprises appear to be quite flexible and mobile geographically. This could be attributed to their response to changes in market opportunities or to the pressures that they face. In the later case, this mobility reduces their incentive to invest in workers training, fixed capital and market/customer development. Roughly 14% of the sample of firms started operations in another governorate, with the majority of mobile firms locating in Sana'a, Aden and Taiz. A number of firms also have the capacity to adjust fixed assets, contracts with workers, locations and product lines as well as move back and forth across the boundaries of formality (Table 3.3). Firms now located in Hadramout are less likely to have started in a different governorate, whereas firms now located in Hodeidah are more likely to have started in a different governorate.[55] Furthermore, small firms in industry, on average, have less than one permanent *paid* employee, with family members making up the bulk of the work effort.

TABLE 3.3: DISTRIBUTION OF RELOCATED FIRMS IN YEMEN

Location of Start-up	Location Now					
	Sana'a	Aden	Taiz	Hodeidah	Hadramout	Total
Dhamar, Ibb, Taiz, Hodeidah, Mahweet	19	12	6	7	3	47
Sana'a, Sadda, Marib, Al-Jouf, Hajjah, Amran	11	7	7	9	2	36
Hadramout, Al-Mahra, Shabwah	1	2			1	4
Aden, Lahj, Al-Beida, Al-Dhaleh, Abyan	16	4	10	6	1	37
Total	47	25	23	22	7	124

Source: Results of the Private Sector Survey undertook by the World Bank in November 2001.

The structure of private sector activity in Yemen suggests the presence of significant barriers to growth in value added and specialization of firms. The large number of very small formal enterprises and very large firms (low numbers of medium sized companies) combined with a more significant tendency for large firms to report barriers to growth suggest that while entry into the formal sector may be relatively easy, profitable expansion may be limited by high levels of risk and uncertainty, administrative hurdles, infrastructure inadequacies, excessive competition and weak firm capacity. This is further underscored by the behavior of existing large firms, which are characterized by significant internalization of activities and services, namely electricity generation, transport, distribution and training as in the case of the largest firms. In other words, profitable market opportunities and services complementary with expanding production are either non-existent (missing) for SMEs or access is highly restricted and/or prohibitively costly. This effectively raises costs of production, and in effect the minimum efficient size for profitable firms in the private sector. High transaction costs related to insufficient mechanisms for contract enforcement, resolution of commercial disputes creates an environment of general legal uncertainty furthering limiting growth potential (Box 3.3).

BOX 3.3: LARGE FIRMS IN YEMEN INTERNALIZE RISK (CONGLOMERATION)

The Hayel Saeed Anam Group in Yemen is one of the most powerful trading conglomerates in Yemen with activities ranging from transport to manufacturing. The company is a private limited liability located in Taiz with roughly 15,000 workers and activities in domestic and foreign raw material purchases, agro foods such as creamery butter, construction materials, as well as consumer goods, industrial production and banking services. Typical of larger firms in Yemen, the Saeed Group demonstrates very effective in-house organization of all transport and distribution needs as well as in-house training of workers.

The benefits of conglomeracy include **reduced instability and uncertainty,** namely the ability for firms to diversify profit flows, **achieve efficiency gains from synergy** such as branching into related produces which may be distributed or marketed together and **new entry** provided it is achieved by international expansion or a "toe hold" acquisition. However, evidence from developed countries suggests, that conglomeration activities among firms may have adverse effects on domestic competition. When large firms confront each other more frequently in outside markets they tend to compete less fiercely in the local market. Conglomeracy is also often associated with reciprocity or the use by a firm of its buying power to promote its sales; I'll buy from you if you buy from me. The effect of this firm behavior may also be to lessen price competition as non-price factors become controlling. Cross subsidization may also disadvantage rivals and distort capital flows.

---

[55] This was evident by multivariate logistic regression analysis [see Banerje and McLeish (2002)].

Private Sector Environment and Governance

Governance problems are perhaps the most evident and important barrier to the development of the private sector, and an impediment to the growth of the size of firms. In general, Yemeni firms face a lack of profitable opportunities, and weak capacity for expansion in product markets. Yet, larger and older firms tend to be more successful, owning their own land and engaging in export activities. One reason for that appears to be the ability of these firms to use their own extensive informal networks. By bypassing formal marketing institutions and creating integrated firm structures, they can bypass the governance and institutional failures in Yemen's business environment. However, these opportunities are restricted to a few groups in the country, and thus the poor functioning of formal market-supporting institutions is a barrier to the successful growth of many new entrants into Yemeni business.[56]

As shown in a survey of Yemeni firms in late 2001, poor governance manifests itself in a number of ways in Yemen: (i) corruption and inefficiency in the interaction of public officials and private businesses; (ii) ineffective or absent market-promoting institutions, such as those enforcing contracts (courts, tribunals etc.) or regulating information flows (e.g., about creditworthiness), and (iii) poor performance of the public sector in terms of delivering essential services (Table 3.4). But this suggests that there is considerable scope to remove the constraints to growth for new small and medium sized firms, by creating formal institutional alternatives to the informal arrangements possessed by the few successful firms. The keys to opening up small and medium firm growth in Yemen seems to lie in developing ways to allow smaller and newer firms access to formal alternatives to the informal and exclusionary mechanisms used by the older and larger firms.

Figure 3.2: Aggregate Governance Indicators: Yemen
Percentile Rankings

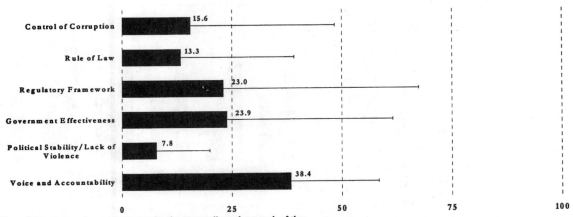

Note: Bars represent mean estimates for the percentile rank on each of the governance indicators. The thin vertical lines represent standard errors around these estimates.

Source: Kaufmann, Kraay and Zoido-Lobaton (1999 b).

---

56 "Market-supporting institutions" are rules, enforcement mechanisms and organizations promoting market transactions by transmitting information, enforcing contracts and managing the degree of competition. Formal institutions that perform these functions range from judicial systems and competition laws, to credit-rating agencies and land titles. See World Bank (2002).

TABLE 3.4: EFFICIENCY OF BUREAUCRATIC TRANSACTIONS IN YEMEN
(Number of days delay to get/deal with:)

Days	Connect to Public Services		Get Licenses and Permits		Deal with Tax Authorities		Get Government Contracts		Clear Customs		Buy Land/ Constr. Permit	
	No.	Valid (%)	No.	Valid (%)	No.	Valid (%)	No.	Valid (%)	No.	Valid (%)	No.	Valid (%)
0	11	3.54	8	1.97	10	2.50	50	45.87	45	23.56	26	23.21
1-5days	87	27.97	158	38.92	170	42.50	7	6.42	77	40.31	15	13.39
6-10days	49	15.76	130	32.02	77	19.25	7	6.42	43	22.51	12	10.71
11-20days	28	9.00	50	12.32	38	9.50	12	11.01	14	7.33	7	6.25
21-50days	69	22.19	36	8.87	45	11.25	7	6.42	7	3.66	17	15.18
51-100days	39	12.54	15	3.69	35	8.75	18	16.51	3	1.57	20	17.86
>100days	28	9.00	9	2.22	25	6.25	8	7.34	2	1.05	15	13.39
Total	311	100	406	100	400	100	109	100	191	100	112	100
Mean	30.28		12.62		21.52		26.23		6.30		30.50	
Median	15		7		7		2		3		10	

Sources: Data from the World Bank Private Sector Survey, November 2001.

Governance has been shown, in a wide variety of studies, to significantly influence development outcomes. Corruption, in particular, has a destructive effect on investment and economic growth rates.[57] By contrast, greater enforcement of property rights, stronger rule of law and efficient government service delivery promotes investment and economic growth.[58] These links between governance measures and development hold not only for traditional economic indicators, but are also well recognized for other development outcomes, including infant mortality, literacy and equality of income growth.[59] In Yemen, governance performance is weak, and that would affect investment and growth. Figure 3.3 shows how, in a major international study, Yemen ranked compared with 188 countries on 6 dimensions of governance.[60] In all but one of the categories, Yemen ranks in the bottom 25% of countries. On control of corruption, Yemen ranks only in the 15th percentile, and its rankings for rule of law and political stability/lack of violence indicators are significantly lower. Even relative to the 19 countries in the Middle East and North Africa region, Yemen's performance on governance indicators is poor.[61] In political stability and lack of violence, only Iraq and Algeria rate lower than Yemen. Out of 19 countries, Yemen ranks 15th in government effectiveness, 14th in regulatory framework, and 16th in both rule of law and corruption. Only in voice and accountability does Yemen perform

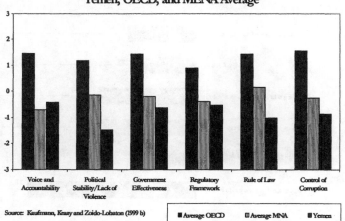

Figure 3.3: Governance Indicators: Yemen, OECD, and MENA Average

Source: Kaufmann, Kraay and Zoido-Lobaton (1999 b)

■ Average OECD   ▥ Average MNA   ■ Yemen

---

[57] For example: Tanzi and Davoodi (1997), Johnson, *et. al.* (1999), Kaufmann *et al.* (1999) and Kaufmann, *et al.* (1999 b).

[58] Kaufmann, Kraay and Zoido-Lobaton (1999).

[59] For example, Kaufmann, *et. al.* (1999).

[60] Kaufmann, *et. al.* (1999). Aggregate governance indicators are based upon over 300 individual indicators from two types of sources: expert polls, and cross country surveys of residents. The authors apply a latent variable model to estimate a common element in each of the 6 categories of governance.

[61] Algeria, Bahrain, Djibouti, Egypt, Iran, Iraq, Jordan, Kuwait, Lebanon, Libya, Morocco, Oman, Qatar, Saudi Arabia, Syria, Tunisia, UAE, West Bank Gaza and Yemen.

relatively better, ranking 6th out of the 19 MENA countries.

Within the Yemeni private sector as well, governance concerns are identified as extremely significant. In the recent private sector survey in Yemen, 82% of firms identified corruption as a major obstacle to the profitable expansion of Yemeni firms. And more than half identified constraints in the administrative, regulatory and legal frameworks in which firms operate, and current gaps in the physical infrastructure (electricity) upon which firms depend for production and distribution of goods and services (Figure 3.4 and Annex Table 13).

Overall, the greatest concerns in the Yemeni business sector seemed to be in two areas: institutional/administrative problems (corruption, taxes, smuggling/dumping, dispute settlement); and volatility/uncertainty (about macro and other policies, and about crime and disorder). To a slightly lesser extent infrastructure and input issues (electricity, access to land) are also perceived to be problems. Relatively few firms, on the other hand, identified telecommunication problems or labor regulations as moderate to severe barriers to expansion.[62]

Figure 3.4: Obstacles to Business and Profitable Expansion
(% of firms indicating moderate to very severe constraints: valid responses)

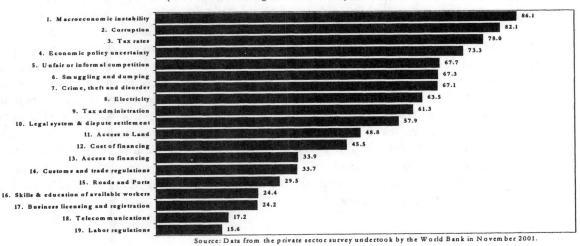

Source: Data from the private sector survey undertook by the World Bank in November 2001.

Entry Costs

According to the survey results, the median time to establish a new business is 3 months (mean 4.8 months). Each connection to infrastructure services and contact with licensing authorities takes a median of 1 month (mean between 1.6 and 2.2 months). Electricity connection emerges as a particularly large barrier in terms of time and costs. Firms report significant unofficial payments to establish a business. Median unofficial

---

[62]   Similar trends emerge when considering the firms' perception of the *importance* of the problem. When asked to identify the most critical obstacle, most firms chose electricity and tax rates, followed by macroeconomic instability, smuggling and dumping, corruption and access to land.

payments are between 12% and 60% of median official payments and are highest for licensing and permits (see Annex Table 15).[63]

TABLE 3.5: RANK 1 OBSTACLE BY FIRM SIZE
(Percent of Firms ranking Obstacle as No. 1).

Small			Medium			Large		
Rank	Obstacle	%	Rank	Obstacle	%	Rank	Obstacle	%
1	Electricity	19.3	1	Tax rates	17.4	1	Smuggling/dumping	23.8
2	Tax rate	18.4	2	Electricity	15.5	2	Macroeconomic instability	12.9
3	Macroeconomic instability	15.0	3	Macroeconomic instability	11.6	3	Corruption	11.9
4	Smuggling/dumping	9.6	4	Smuggling/dumping	10.3	4	Tax rates	8.9
5	Access to land	9.0	5	Corruption	7.1	5	Electricity	8.9

Source: Data from the private sector survey undertook by the World Bank in November 2001.

Delays and Informal Payments for Ongoing Operations

Bureaucratic interactions for ongoing operations also involve significant delays and informal payments (see Annex Table 16). Delays vary significantly by Governorate, although the ranking of regions varies depending upon the question. Aden and Hadramout report greater delays in purchasing land and getting construction permits but fewer delays with tax collectors. For the case of government contracts, services and permits, delays also vary by firm size (with larger firms report greater delays). Of those who responded on informal payments for bureaucratic interaction, a significant majority indicated the need to take informal payments for these interactions (Figure 3.5). The location of the firm matters; firms in Hodeidah are significantly more likely to make informal payments for permits, tax and customs, whereas firms in Aden and Taiz are less likely to make informal payments for customs. Larger and older firms report a higher incidence of making informal payments than smaller firms. However, evidence suggests that corruption does not have an efficiency payoff. Firms making informal payments do not experience fewer delays in bureaucratic transactions than firms who do not make such payments.[64] Therefore, the evidence that older and larger firms are more likely to make unofficial payments may be less a result of firm experience or ability in expediting services and more about prominent firms attracting unwanted attention from public officials.

Quality of Infrastructure

Firms report that the average number of days of power disruption is as high as 75 (the median is 30 days). By comparison, in Morocco the average incidence of power disruption is 16 times per year with a median of 12. For water, on average Yemeni firms experience 82 days of inadequate supply (with a median of 6 days), whereas the frequency of telephone disruption is considerably lower, with an average of 4 days. Larger firms tend to report greater difficulties with nearly every aspect of the business environment with the exception of policy uncertainty. Larger firms view themselves as having more influence over policy formulation. Access to and cost of financing does not appear to be a significant

---

[63] For details, see Banerji and McLeish (2002). Furthermore, non-parametric tests indicate that these unofficial payments are statistically significant.

[64] Banerji and McLeish (2002) provide such evidence using both t-test and non-parametric tests.

barrier to firm expansion, similar to other MENA countries, but is a more important issue for new firms, in conjunction with access to legal and dispute settlement.[65]

Figure 3.5: Incidence of Irregular Payments
% of Firms Indicating Informal Payments (Valid Responses)

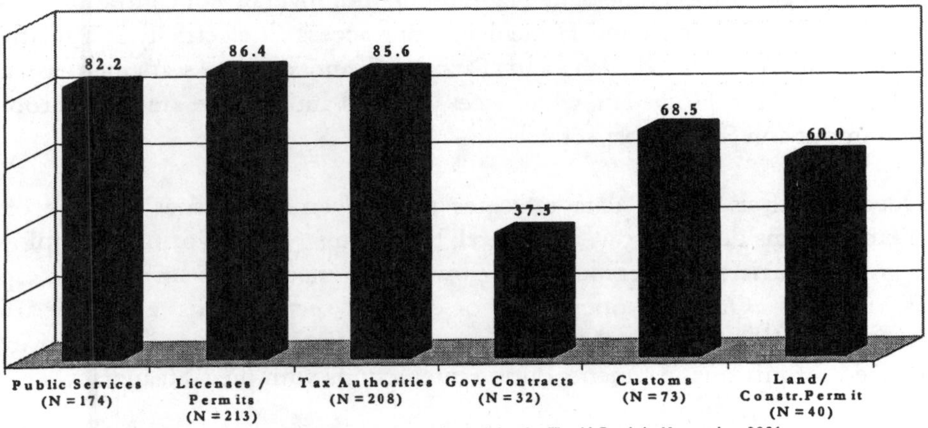

Source: Data from the private sector survey undertook by the World Bank in November 2001.

Access to Land

Yemeni entrepreneurs and investors are inhibited in terms of access to commercially viable and reasonably priced land due to shortages created by government largesse and real estate speculation. According to the recent survey, the majority of firms rent land (68%), and inadequate access to land appears to be a significant obstacle to firm expansion in Aden, Taiz and Hadramout. The majority of firms which own land are large firms, although land ownership is not insurance against multiple claims: nearly 4% of the sample firms reported problems with multiple claims on their land. Land disputes are also costly to revolve, on average firms spend more than one year resolving claims in court and the majority of land disputes are handled through formal channels as opposed to mediation.[66]

Security and Violence

About 28% of firms reported at least one violent incidence in their neighborhood during the previous three months: 9.4% of respondents reported one incident, 4.2% reported two incidents and 14.2% reported that violent incidents took place more than twice. The incidence of reported violence varies significantly cross regions Firms in Taiz and Sana'a are significantly more likely to record violence in their neighborhood. Manufacturing and foreign owned firms are more likely also to report violent incidence in the neighborhood.[67] Lack of security is a contributing factor in the segmentation of markets, the smallness of business and the dispersion of business across regions.

---

[65] About 53% of all firms surveyed do not have a bank account. The provision of credit by banks is, therefore, very low. About 12% of valid responses (those who have banks account) received credit from banks. Resources from within the firms are the most common source of both short-term and investment finance.

[66] Overall, of all the firms that have invested outside Yemen, half of them did so because of more attractive foreign opportunities, while one-quarters of those firms said that they invested aboard due to obstacles in the domestic market.

[67] For details, see Banerji and McLeish (2002).

Regional Differences

However, within regions, there are some important differences in terms of where obstacles are more severe. The severity of all major obstacles appears to be fairly constant across Sana'a, Aden, Taiz, Hodeidah, Hadramout, but overall concentration of obstacles appears to be higher in Sana'a and Hodeidah.[68] But access to electricity is a relatively more severe obstacle in Aden, Hodeidah, and Taiz; legal and dispute settlement is more of a problem in Sana'a, Taiz, Hodeidah; while access to land and finance are more problematic in Aden, Hadramout and Sana'a, respectively.

Deeper analysis of the data indicates that governance issues may be one of the reasons Yemeni firms do not grow. In general, large firms (with 10 or more employees) tend to report greater barriers to operation and growth than medium or small firms, especially in the areas of taxes. Ongoing operations of private sector firms are also affected by governance problems, increasing their costs and decreasing efficiency. One clear example of this is the need for informal payments during interactions with the bureaucracy.

Yemeni firms' perception of policy uncertainty may be affected by the fact that they have relatively little voice in policy formulation. Well over 60% of responding firms identified social and tribal influences as a major influence on policy formulation, more than half identified "key private players" (Figure 3.6). Less than 15% of respondents identified their own firm as having a voice in the policy formulation process, with most of these being the larger firms (more than 100 employees).

Figure 3.6: Influence over Policy Formulation in Yemen
(% firms indicating somewhat or very influential: valid responses)

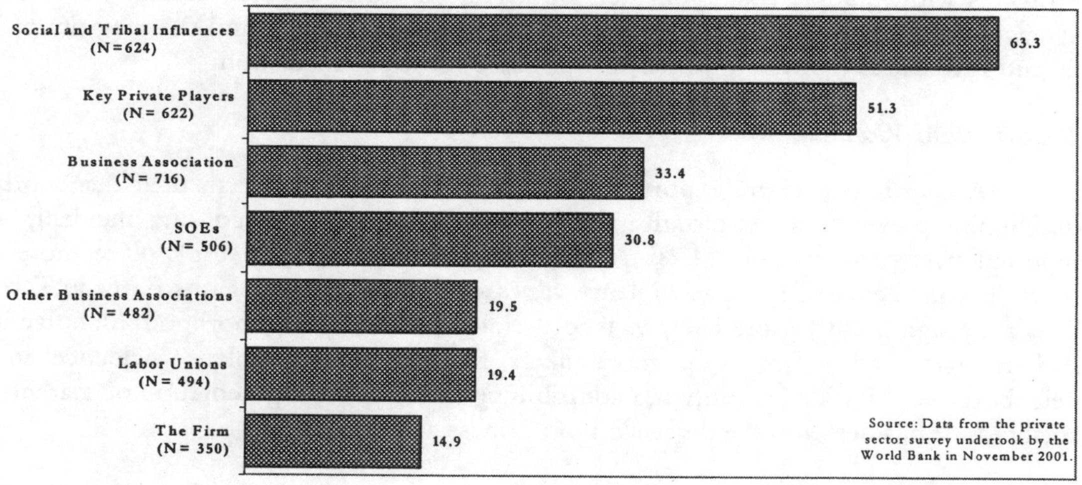

Social and Tribal Influences (N=624)	63.3
Key Private Players (N= 622)	51.3
Business Association (N= 716)	33.4
SOEs (N= 506)	30.8
Other Business Associations (N= 482)	19.5
Labor Unions (N= 494)	19.4
The Firm (N= 350)	14.9

Source: Data from the private sector survey undertook by the World Bank in November 2001.

TOWARD A REFORM AGENDA FOR PRIVATE SECTOR DEVELOPMENT

In Yemen, the largest sectors—food processing, oil-related, and construction related industries—exist because they either meet basic domestic needs or because they reflect other activities in the economy. So there is not much scope for picking winners and focusing on

---

68   Taiz and Hodeidah also tend to experience more frequent disruptions in electricity and water services.

developing them. The best way to foster growth in the private sector is to create an environment where Yemeni (and foreign) investors can select their own areas of entry and then to allow their businesses to grow. The development of the private sector in Yemen is best achieved by reducing and eliminating the existing barriers to the growth of firms. While such a broad institutional development agenda is probably not going to be achieved within a very short time period, a focus on addressing the problems can yield results over the medium term. This is, for example, evidenced by the quick development of the successful countries in Central Europe, such as Slovenia, Hungary and Poland, which put a strong and credible emphasis on restoring and improving market institutions and governance during the 1990s. A slightly different approach, offering incentives and lowering regulatory barriers to all exporters, was successful in helping Mauritius grow rapidly (Box 3.4).

BOX 3.4: MAURITIUS: ENCLAVE MANUFACTURING AS A WAY OF DEVELOPING A MANUFACTURING SECTOR

One approach towards diversifying away from oil has been to promote open trade policies on the ground by developing a competitive, export-oriented enclave manufacturing sector. Since 1970, Mauritius has built a large and competitive clothing industry within its Export Processing Zone (EPZ). The Mauritius EPZ regime differs from other LDC Free Trade Zones in that it is not a 'zone' physically separated from the rest of the economy, but a system of incentives granted to firms exporting 100% of their output (with certain minor exceptions). Firms anywhere on the island enjoy equal footing export policies including free trade status based on the duty (and indirect tax) exemption system.

Integrated strategies guaranteed equal footing export policies and infrastructure for all export activities. These were implemented through the Mauritius Export Development and Investment Authority, the Development Bank of Mauritius, the Export Credit Guarantee Scheme, and the Export Credit Insurance Scheme. The government also encouraged private sector initiatives in FTZ development and management through measures such as the Industrial Building Investment Scheme. Attempts were made to maximize the gains from foreign collaboration and upgrade the industrial structure in a diversified and more skill-intensive direction. For example, the Export Services Zone Scheme of 1981 and a recent offshore banking center were designed to diversify FTZ export industries. The new Industrial Training Strategy aims at speeding up industrial skill acquisition.

In Yemen, many of the reforms needed have already begun. Key among these are the reform of the civil service and judicial reform initiatives. Over the medium term, the agenda for the private sector has to include a broad array of actions that address the four major areas of problems identified by Yemeni firms: policy uncertainty, the lack of governance/market institutions, poor public service provision, and inadequate financial intermediation.

Reducing Policy Uncertainty

There are three levels of uncertainty for firms, especially small and medium firms, in Yemen: uncertainty about the macro-fiscal environment, uncertainty about the course and sequence of structural policies, and uncertainty due to the lack of market information. Separate sets of practices will need to be adopted to address each of these.

Macroeconomic policies influence private sector activity through the level and prices of firms' outputs, the prices of inputs, the interest firms pay on debt, wages paid and exchange rates under which firms operate. When prices are stable and external payments are sustainable, the private sector can more easily plan future output, levels and investment. In the case of Yemen, the perception of private sector firms about macroeconomic instability may be at odds with reality. All macroeconomic indicators are more stable now than 5 years ago although inflation remains quite volatile. The held perception may be due to lack of transparency (in terms of budget and policies), lack of medium-term orientation in policies and unreliable statistics. Moreover, a major source of <u>macro-fiscal uncertainty</u> appears to be volatility in government revenues due to commodity price fluctuations and patterns of fiscal spending. Private sector agents in turn are wary of the government's ability to finance its deficit, and tend to defer longer term capital investment decisions or engage in short term, lower risk activities at the expense of more productive investments. What is needed at the macroeconomic level is to continue Yemen's concentrated and sustained effort toward prudent macroeconomic management, promoting open trade policies and a competitive exchange rate. This would be especially important in times of lower oil prices. Countries such as Indonesia and Chile were able to curb the deleterious effects of oil rent by retaining relatively open trade policies and market incentives for most investment allocation.[69]

Structural policy uncertainty can be reduced, in turn, by a more transparent, inclusive and open policymaking process as a means to reduce the uncertainties faced by the private sector in Yemen. In Singapore, for example, private citizens serve as directors on government statutory boards and as members of ad hoc advisory committees. They review policies and programs, making recommendations for official consideration. In addition, the government regularly invites chambers of commerce, trade associations and professional societies to submit their views on specific issues. Transparency as to the government's plans also helps. In Yemen, one initiative that points the way is the steering committee, formed in early 1999, that is bringing private firms and government officials together to review legal obstacles to private investment, and to recommend changes to the regulatory structure and administrative procedures for trade and investment. Again, the prompt and wide publication and publicizing of the government's reform agenda, as for example embodied in the PRSP, can also greatly help the process.

Finally, because of Yemen's less-developed market institutions, firms face specific uncertainties due to lack of information. These include the inability to identify markets; insecurity and unenforceability of contracts; and the lack of specialized business skills, such as accounting and bookkeeping, marketing, exporting. Such factors increase the uncertainty faced by the firms about its future earnings and prospects, and once again induce them to indulge in low-risk, short-term activities.[70] Reducing such <u>firm-specific uncertainties</u> would require a range of institution-building, and the need to make available planning and business resources to the firms. Institutionalizing firm linkages in the form of subcontracting and franchising can provide additional mechanisms for knowledge and technology transfer, as well as for improving product quality and introducing new products to the local market. The experience of the East Asian countries suggests that subcontracting from large firms to first and second tier SMEs provided opportunities for information sharing, technology transfer and coordination of management and marketing skills in a mentoring environment.

---

[69] Auty (2002).

[70] Foreign firms tend to locate in particular countries on the basis of factors such as proximity to input and output markets, quality of infrastructure, low labor costs, fiscal incentives and a qualified workforce. In the case of Yemen, recent surveys of foreign investors indicate that location for example, is an important asset for the Yemeni economy but enthusiasm to invest is tempered by a lack of certainty with regard to property rights, and commercial dispute settlement procedures (see FIAS (1997)].

Improving Governance and Market Institutions

In Yemen, private sector development can be greatly helped by improved governance (especially in bureaucratic-private sector interactions) as well as the development of formal, market-based institutions. Among the many areas in which action is needed, three are paramount: enhanced accountability of the government and the civil service, better legal and contract-enforcement systems, and reduced regulatory barriers.

Strengthening the <u>accountability of the public sector</u> in its role in regulating private activity is one of the most important steps in allowing Yemeni firms, especially those that are small, to grow. In the 2001 survey of private firms, more than 80% of all firms responded that corruption was a significant problem, with firms in Sana'a and Hodeidah being the most concerned about the issue (Figure 3.7). As reported by the firms, informal payments are almost essential to obtain public services, licenses and permits, and when dealing with the tax authorities. To a lesser extent, informal payments were reported as needed for customs and land/construction permits.

Figure 3.7: Percentage of Firms
Identifying Corruption as a Moderate
to Severe Obstacle

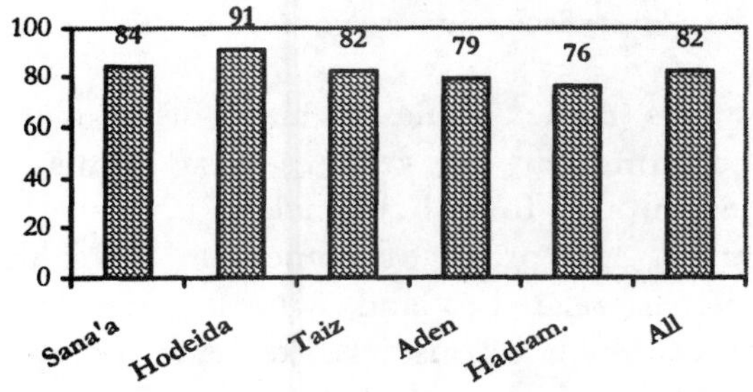

Figure 3.8: Percentage of Firms
Identifying Tax Administration as a
Moderate to Severe Obstacle

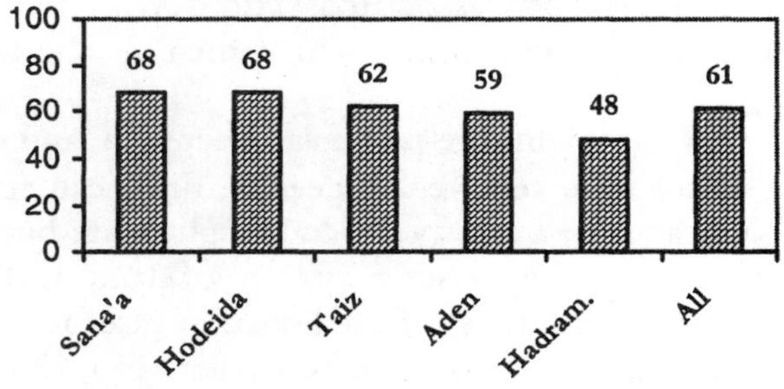

Source: Private Sector Survey, November 2001.

Source: Private Sector Survey, November 2001.

Again, for example, the Yemeni tax administration has been singled out by investors and firms as creating a substantial obstacle to growth. In the survey, over three out of five firms identified tax administration as a major barrier to growth (Figure 3.8). There are clear regional differences, with, once again, the extent of the problem being highest in Sana'a and Hodeidah, and the lowest in Hadramout. In addition, foreign investors have traditionally described the tax system as highly complicated and corrupt, demonstrated by anecdotal evidence that different tax officers frequently visit a firm to collect the same tax (sometimes even on the same day), leaving investors with little choice but to pay the tax again or to bribe the tax collector. Delay is another form of soliciting bribes, as tax collectors can delay in examining the accounting files of the firm for up to 2 years if investors refuse to offer bribes.

Addressing these issues would require extensive civil service reform and administrative accountability measures, some of which have already been initiated by the government. A drastic reduction in the number of civil servants overseeing the private sector, and clarification of their roles and responsibilities, is a clear need. At the same time, there is a need for increased administrative accountability mechanisms, including procurement reform and better auditing and oversight. Finally, as the total wage bill decreases due to a decreasing number of civil servants, civil service pay has to be increased to lower the incentives to be corrupt, while better monitoring and punishment of offenders also serves the same purpose.

Recent studies from other developed and developing countries suggest that new, small private firms are more dependent on the functioning of formal legal systems in commercial litigation. Yet, a surprisingly large number of firms in Yemen rely on informal mediation to resolve payment disputes, which while more expedient, is not necessarily more efficient or predictable than formal court appeals. In the survey, 58% of them cite it as a major obstacle to business (Figure 3.9). Thus, better formal legal and contract-enforcement systems are needed to reduce the high cost and uncertainty associated with informal dispute resolution in Yemen.

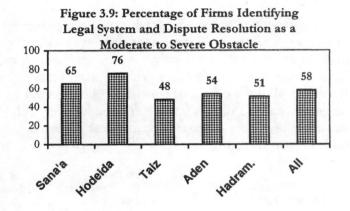

Figure 3.9: Percentage of Firms Identifying Legal System and Dispute Resolution as a Moderate to Severe Obstacle

Source: Private Sector Survey, November 2001.

Problems are particularly acute in land disputes (Annex Table 14). Land disputes are also costly to resolve, on average firms can spend more than one year resolving claims in court and the majority of land disputes are handled through formal channels as opposed to mediation. The existing system of land registration and proof of ownership is highly ineffective and most of the litigation cases in Yemen are related to land ownership disputes. Land registration is governed by Law No. 12 of 1976 which is considered to be ambiguous and ineffective, contributing to the existing system in which registration of deeds by a registered public officer and notification to the registry testifies to land ownership.

There are two areas of problems in terms of dispute resolution in Yemen—first, with the judicial administrative and institutional process itself, and second, with outmoded and insufficient laws. In particular, the main problems currently facing the Yemeni judiciary include: (i) poor legal and administrative performance of the judiciary and administrative personnel due to lack of motivation and/or lack of requisite education and skills; (ii) absence of proper administrative systems (file keeping, registration of contracts, regulation of fees, etc.); (iii) dilapidated court buildings; and, above all (iv) a lack of probity at all levels.

In 1997, the government implemented a strategy for legal and judicial reform that called for an increase in judicial independence, an emphasis on probity and integrity of the judicial body, an enhanced role for judicial oversight bodies such as the Supreme Judiciary Council and the Judicial Inspection Board, improved court facilities, improved court administration, and a training program for judges. The success of these efforts would determine to a large extent whether the formal system dispute resolution would see improved use. In the mean time, Yemen could experiment with alternative dispute resolution mechanisms, which have been successful in many developing countries (Box 3.5).

In terms of legislation, new laws, particularly modern commercial codes, will be required as part of the development of a workable legal system and to support a market based economy. Specific areas include the financial sector (secured transactions and real and personal property registers), insolvency, bankruptcy and others. The Government is already tackling several under-served areas, such as privatization and banking regulations. Current reforms to address the shortcomings in the Land law include formation of an inter-ministerial committee, which is working on streamlining procedures for proving clear title and registration for all properties to be privatized.

BOX 3.5: FAST-TRACK INSTITUTIONAL MECHANISMS FOR LEGAL REFORM (TANZANIA AND BANGLADESH)

In Tanzania, a commercial court was established with support from government, private business and international donors as a specialized division of the High Court to accelerate the process of building a legal and judicial system to support market reforms. By imposing greater selectivity and simplified procedures, the court has effectively cut the average time to disposition from 22 to 3 months. The Commercial Court has jurisdiction over cases involving amounts greater than about $12,500 and has a higher fee structure than the general division of the High Court. This discourages frivolous litigation and prevents appeals, a common source of additional cost and delay.

In Bangladesh, the Maduirpur Legal Aid Association (MLAA) a Bangladeshi NGO has established a mediation structure in rural areas to deliver dispute settlement services for women. The local MLAA meet twice a month to hear village disputes, provide mediation outside the court system, free of charge. Nearly 15% of disputes deal with property and land disputes and plaintiffs prefer the mediation systems since it is locally administered, transparent to the community and quick to render judgment with a decision typically made within 45 days of the filing.

Source: World Bank (2002)

Private sector firms tend to face burdensome <u>regulatory and administrative hurdles</u> procedures—in setting up businesses, and in commencing/expanding business operations. A number of entrepreneurs cite the licensing process and procedures as a major hindrance to firm establishment and growth, and may abandon the process halfway or simply neglect to have their license renewed on any annual basis. Furthermore, this licensing procedure does not prevent the need for dealing with individual government departments and ministries with regard to infrastructure access. Business facilitating entities such as the GIA effectively act as a port of entry for investors, but are not actively engaged as a one stop shop for facilitating the investment process and can provide no guarantees that firms will have accelerated or friendly dealings with other government agencies responsible for the nature of their activities.

Thus, improved coordination among government agencies, perhaps aided by the elimination of investment licensing, is an important step towards the development of private sector activity. Another way to achieve this is to create a 'one stop' or 'first stop' shop for potential entrepreneurs and business owners. The GIA could effectively serve as the first stop shop for potential and current business owners, being the single portal for information on licensing and permits required to start and expand a business in Yemen. Formal complaint and appeals procedures attached to this regulatory administration would also provide a mechanism for the transmission of vital information and feedback about the impact of government policies.

Improving the Quality of Public Services

Yemeni firms are also hampered by relatively poor access to infrastructure, including electricity and transportation. Promoting greater competition and efficiency in these areas would, therefore, facilitate private sector growth. Yemen's electricity generating capacity is inadequate for the country's needs—as is evident from the number of firms citing it as a significant problem (Figure 3.10). In addition to the cities surveyed, there are large areas of the country such as Mukalla, which are not connected to the national grid serving Aden, Sana'a and the northern cities. Service is characterized by fluctuating voltage supplies and constant blackouts, with adverse consequences for production and investment. The majority of medium and large firms have back-up generators, which adds significantly to production costs. Larger firms frequently have to assume the cost of installing electrical lines to their project sites, a process that can take up to 12 months. Clearly, there is a need to accelerate the ongoing efforts by the government to introduce greater competition for the electricity market.   Source: Private Sector Survey, November 2001.

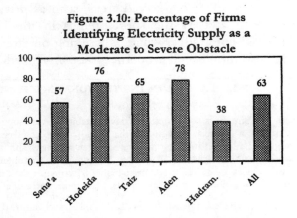

Figure 3.10: Percentage of Firms Identifying Electricity Supply as a Moderate to Severe Obstacle

The road transport system in Yemen is limited (Chapter 2), critically affecting the internal distribution of goods and inhibiting the development of markets for local products. Incomplete connections to ports and airports affect the ability of industries to export, and impede the movement of people. In addition, the continued division of most of the country along tribal lines imposes additional costs on internal trade.

The trucking sector, in particular, has been controlled by a private cartel, which keeps transport costs high through price fixing and barriers to entry as well as by preventing private firms and traders from providing their own transport. A draft Surface Transportation Law approved by the cabinet in 1999 calls for establishment of the General Land Transport Authority to be put in charge of granting trucking licenses and posting suggested tariffs. In addition, by-laws, which superficially regulate the trucking sector, have been issued allowing any trucker to obtain a license for operation valid anywhere in Yemen.

Improving Financial Intermediation

The financial system in Yemen is weaker than in most other MENA countries. Its structural weaknesses and inefficiencies are reflected in low intermediation ratios, high interest rate spreads, and the prevalence of cash as the principal medium of exchange. Wide spreads between lending and deposit rates, and low profitability among banks, reflect a lack of interest of banks to grant credit or mobilize deposits. Large non-performing portfolios worsen the situation. The 2001 private sector

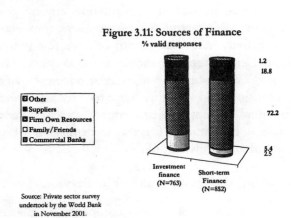

Figure 3.11: Sources of Finance
% valid responses

☒ Other
■ Suppliers
☒ Firm Own Resources
☐ Family/Friends
■ Commercial Banks

Investment finance (N=763)

Short-term Finance (N=852)

1.2
18.8
72.2

Source: Private sector survey undertook by the World Bank in November 2001.

survey found that a large number of firms (481 or 53% of the total respondents) did not have a bank account. Essentially, the Yemeni banking sector is characterized by high concentration of credit to a small number of companies and groups, insider lending, and prevalent use of overdraft facilities. The survey found considerable variation among the firms: firms in Sana'a and Hodeidah, large firms, and older firms were all significantly more likely to have a bank account. In the absence of formal credit, private and informal sources of credit are the only recourse for most Yemeni firms. Resources from within the firm are the most common source of both short term and investment finance (Figure 3.11), followed by suppliers, the family and friends and lastly commercial banks.

One reason why banks have been reluctant to lend to smaller firms is the absence of information about their credit history and business prospects. Recent financial sector reforms have helped change the incentives for the banks, by removing Government controls on lending and strengthening banking supervision at the CBY. The banking law of 1998, implemented from 1999, established a solid legal basis for the CBY to set limits on credit concentration and insider lending. With regard to overdraft facilities, which account for roughly 90% of bank credits, the CBY introduced a new system of classifying exposures, with the intent of helping banks to identify and remedy weak credit facilities at an early stage. The CBY has also instituted a notification system, under which banks are notified whether loan applicants are delinquent to other banks. However, despite these positive changes in the legal and regulatory framework for banking, implementation and enforcement remain weak. Furthermore, regulatory strengthening and liberalization of interest rate regulations have not resulted in an increase in lending to the private sector.

BOX 3.6: YEMEN'S PRIVATIZATION PROGRAM

Yemen's privatization program was initiated in early 1995 and contributed to the privatization of more than 60 small enterprises between 1994 and 1997. The implementation of the program has been conducted in a somewhat ad hoc manner, with significant involvement of ministries each of which established internal committees to privatize or liquidate enterprises under their jurisdiction. After the Privatization Law was passed in 1999, privatization procedures were organized and unified and a Technical Privatization Office was established to ensure implementation of standardized and transparent privatization transactions and procedures. However at present the privatization program has been stalled, as in many countries by fears of political reprisal and employment losses.

The continued small size of the banking sector reflects far deeper structural and institutional obstacles.[71] Weaknesses in the legal and judicial framework, lack of proper accounting and auditing standards and disclosure practices, and a scarcity of banking and financial skills remain significant impediments. In particular, there is pressing need to improve the functioning of commercial courts and the judicial processes for recovery of bank and other debts. Accounting and auditing practices—for which no standards have been set in Yemen—are urgently needed both in order to allow creditors some measure of confidence in clients' financial positions and to provide the entire private sector some measure of protection from the widely reported corruption in the tax authority. Thus,

---

[71] Most Yemeni banks are owner by a few large groups that are not only the main borrowers from their respective banks but also many of the wieners are directly involved in the operations of these banks. Some of these groups are not profitable and they are largely responsible for the high ratio of non-performing to total loans in the privately owned Yemeni commercial banks. This practice has the effect of crowding out lending opportunities to other potential borrowers.

improved financial intermediation will only accompany the governance and institutional reforms outlined earlier, which are central to creating an improved climate for business to flourish in Yemen.

CHAPTER 4:
EXTERNAL TRADE SECTOR AND EXPORT COMPETITIVENESS

INTRODUCTION AND SUMMARY OF FINDINGS

Given Yemen's small internal market, exports have to be the major source of rapid job and income growth. The GoY recognizes the importance of the external sector in its development plans and has made good progress in reforming the trade regime. Yemen is now classified among the most open and trade liberalized countries in the MENA region. Nonetheless, most of Yemen's current non-oil exports remain primary, low value-added products, which also makes economic growth more vulnerable to volatility in price and demand. Yet Yemen has considerable room to improve its export performance, and especially non-oil merchandise exports as well as export of services. While import substitution had provided the initial impetus to Yemen's industrial sector in the 1970s and 1980s, the low incomes of Yemen's relatively small population mean that such a strategy is unlikely to be sustainable in the decade of the 2000s. At the same time, Yemen has the major advantage of location. It is in close proximity to potential markets: the high-income GCC countries, other Arab countries, and the underserved economies in the Horn of Africa. For the last group of countries, Yemen had significant "revealed comparative advantages" in several products.

This Chapter reviews recent developments in the product composition of Yemeni exports, direction of trade and the underlying factors behind the performance of Yemeni exports. It also attempts to ascertain whether export performance could be attributed to developments in world trade, changes in product composition of commodities or to changes in the competitiveness of exports. In addition, the Chapter also analyses the product categories and export markets that have driven export development in Yemen. The analysis in this Chapter is based on UNComTrade data.[72]

The main findings of the chapter are that: (i) despite its low volumes, Yemen's export performance has been relatively good in the post civil war period; (ii) exports are dominated by oil exports with more than 90% of total merchandise exports; (iii) exports have been characterized by significant fluctuations in the 1990's because of heavy dependence on oil exports to concentrated markets, and the base for non-oil exports is very narrow with a few items (e.g., fish and coffee) accounting for the bulk of non-oil exports; (iv) value-added in fish exports is very small in comparison with other fish exporters while coffee export market is dominated by a single country, Saudi Arabia; (v) manufacturing exports are still very small in comparison with similar low income countries and the country's manufacturing export capacity is not fully exploited yet even after substantial reforms to the trade and foreign exchange regimes; and, (vi) constant market share analysis reveals that the growth of Yemen's total exports, and manufacturing exports, in the post civil war period has been mainly driven by growth in world trade while improvements in international competitiveness has been a factor for non-oil commodity export growth.

---

[72] For more detail on the competitiveness analysis in this Chapter , see Someya (2001).

EXPORT PERFORMANCE, DIVERSIFICATION, AND DIRECTION OF TRADE

Export of merchandise goods has been one of the driving forces for Yemen's economic growth, particularly in the second half of 1990s. In fact, more than half of GDP growth was attributed to exports during this period. Yemen's total merchandized exports increased from US$ 2.5 billion in 1999 to US$ 4.1 billion in 2000 making Yemen the 90th largest exporter among 231 countries in the world and one of the largest exporters among low-income countries. Yemen's export performance was impressive with an average growth rate of 5.0% during 1995-1999 (6.3% for 1995-2000), better than the world export growth, which was 4.5% over the same period.

Merchandise exports, however, have been characterized by significant fluctuations, dominance of oil exports, and market concentration. The coefficient of variation of Yemen export growth during 1992-1999 is 1.7; more than twice the corresponding figure of the world export growth of 0.8. On the other hand, oil exports represented more than 95% of total merchandise exports in 2000. Non-oil exports, which accounted for less than 10% of total exports in the 1990s, are dominated by three commodities: fish, coffee, and fruits and vegetables (accounting for more than half of non-oil exports). Fruits and vegetables for regional markets have increased rapidly in the late 1990s, jumping up from US$ 1.5 million in 1995 to US$ 12.3 million in 2000. Manufactured exports account for only 1.1% of total merchandise exports.

BOX 4.1: FISH EXPORTS

Fish is the second largest export item in Yemen generating US$ 49 million in 1999 (2.1% of total exports and 35% of non-oil exports). During 1994-1995, fish exports slowed as a result of the temporary export ban and weak demand in neighboring countries. During 1995-1999, fish exports grew by an impressive annual average of 19% versus a 1.4% growth in total world fish trade. This took place despite the appreciation of fish prices in 1994-1998. Yemen's fish export market is concentrated in three countries: Saudi Arabia, Hong Kong and Thailand (absorbing 74% of total fish exports). Exports to the EU, USA and Japan were limited because Yemen does not meet the sanitary standards requested by these countries. Therefore, most of the fish exports are first exported, or smuggled, to Saudi Arabia, Oman or UAE for re-export to the western countries. Exports to Thailand are growing because of existing and large processing facilities before re-directing processed fish to Japan, EU and the US. Therefore, the observed concentration of fish exports does not mean that the final destinations are concentrated in these markets.

Yemen's fish exports are extremely low value-added. The ratio of processed marine resources in total fish exports for Yemen is 0.004%. The corresponding figures for other fish exporters such as Thailand, China, Morocco and Saudi Arabia are 44%, 34%, 26% and 26% respectively. The world average is 17.3%.

By increasing the value added on fish exports through processing and by improving sanitary standards required by large fish markets such as EU, Japan and USA, there are huge prospects for Yemen to bolster fish exports much more rapidly. For instance, Thailand which itself is endowed with abundant marine resources, actually imports US$ 767 million of raw fish (in which Yemen fish exports account for 1.1%) and exports US$ 2 billion of prepared fish products mainly to Japanese and US markets. The Thai fish export is competitive not only because of comparative advantage in a traditional sense based on factor endowment but also because of the created comparative advantage of large scale fish processing facilities.

Yemen can also increase fish production by fish farming which is currently lacking. In 2000, 23% of world fish production was produced through fish farming (28 million tons out of 122 million tons of total world fish production). Even industrialized countries as USA and Canada are engaged in fish farming for luxurious fish such as tuna. Thailand and Philippines also specialize in shrimp farming, aiming at the Chinese and Japanese markets, in which shrimp accounts for a large share. The advantage of fish farming lies in its capability to adjust to market demand. It gives control over the timing to market fish and to mitigate the fluctuations stemming from price charges.

Source: Someya (2001)

Yemen's exports are dominated not only by a few export items such as petroleum, fish and coffee, but also by a few export markets. The top five countries account for more than two thirds of total exports during the 1990s. The degree of market domination by five countries has even worsened from 70% in 1991 to 83% in 1999. Despite market concentration, Yemen' export partners have changed in last ten years. In 1991, four out of five top destinations of Yemen's exports were Western countries. However, all the five largest export destinations in 1999 were emerging Asian countries. This increasing market concentration towards emerging Asian countries reflects the high degree of vulnerability of exports to the outlook in these emerging markets (Table 4.1).

TABLE 4.1: YEMEN MAIN EXPORT MARKETS (%)

	1991		1995		1999	
1	Germany	30.8	Korea, Rep	23.9	Thailand	27.1
2	United States	14.2	China	17.8	China	23.5
3	France	11.8	Japan	17.2	Korea, Rep.	13.0
4	Austria	7.8	Singapore	12.1	India	11.0
5	Taiwan	5.6	Brazil	7.0	Singapore	8.3
Total		70.2		78.1		92.9

Source: Someya (2001).

The direction of trade for non-oil exports is quite different from total merchandise exports. The GCC, and Saudi Arabia in particular, remain the major destination to Yemen non-oil exports. In addition, a few other non-GCC countries (such as Jordan and Egypt) were among Yemen largest importers for non-oil exports together with a few countries in East Africa such as Ethiopia (Table 4.2). For individual non-oil exports items, Saudi Arabia imported 75% of Yemen coffee exports between 1991-1999, 42% of fish exports in 1999. Similarly, Jordan imported 12.3% of Yemen's fish exports in 1995 and 4.1% in 1999; Oman imported 6% of Yemen fish exports in 1995 and 2% in 1999. For manufactured exports, Ethiopia imported about 15% of Yemen total merchandise exports during 1995-1999, Egypt imported 5% of total manufactured exports in 1995 and Djibouti imported about 3% of total manufactured exports in 1991.

TABLE 4.2: YEMEN MAJOR EXPORT MARKETS FOR NON-OIL EXPORTS, 1991-1998

	1991		1995		1998	
1	Saudi Arabia	19	Saudi Arabia	36	Saudi Arabia	26
2	United Kingdom	11	Italy	7	United States	8
3	France	11	United Kingdom	7	India	7
4	Italy	10	United States	5	Ethiopia	6
5	Belgium-Luxembourg	9	Singapore	5	Hong Kong, Chin	6
6	Malaysia	7	Japan	4	Japan	5
7	Singapore	6	Jordan	4	Italy	4
8	Japan	6	Hong Kong, Chin	3	United Kingdom	4
9	Korea, Rep.	4	India	3	Germany	4
10	United States	2	Korea, Rep.	3	Jordan	3
Total		61		59		53

Source: UNCOMTRADE database.

Relative to other developing countries in the MENA region, competitiveness in the form of export potential is also concentrated in large, older firms, predominantly located in Sana'a, Aden and Hodeidah. Only 3.5% of firms sampled (Chapter 3) are engaged in export activities relative to 56% firms in Morocco where exporters are predominantly new firms entering the market (42% of firms begin exporting after one year) with a clear export focus and new product lines.

EXCHANGE RATE POLICY REFORMS AND COMPETITIVENESS

In July 1990, the exchange rate and trade systems of the former Yemeni republics were unified using the system of the former YAR. To contain the spillover of the growing financial imbalances to the external accounts, a complex system of "hybrid" segmented foreign exchange markets was devised in addition to the adoption of a number of ad hoc administrative measures to curb "speculative" activity and wide-ranging trade restrictions.[73] The forging exchange market was comprised of official and parallel markets. The official market was limited to government external transactions and covered crude oil and petroleum products, official receipts and payments and external debt service payments. It also applied to the allocations of foreign exchange by the CBY to the private sector for imports of wheat, flour, rice and LPG as well as for special purposes such as medical treatment or study aboard. All other external transactions occurred through the parallel market, which was operated by moneychangers and did not have a legal status until January 1993. At that time a law was enacted to establishing regulations for money changing operations including licensing, capital and reporting requirements and which assigned oversight powers to the CBY.

The attempt to defend nominal exchange rates led to sharp appreciation of the real effective exchange rate (REER) in the first half of the 1990s undercutting efforts to contain fiscal and external balances (see Figure 3.4). It became increasingly clear that multiple exchange rates and foreign exchange controls exacerbated the negative impact of external shocks, and in 1993-1994 the authorities took some partial steps to achieve the positive real interest rates and more realistic exchange rates. Faced with a growing gap between the free markers parallel rate and the various official rates in November 1994, the authorities introduced a managed "official parallel market" rate at YR 84 per US dollar, to be guided by an oversight committee of moneychangers and commercial bank representatives under the supervision of the CBY taking into account market indicators. The CBY enforced the offal parallel markets rate by mandating that commercial banks could open letters of credit only of the importer provided documentary evidence that the foreign exchange was purchased at the official parallel rate. This attempt to manage the parallel market failed, however, and by end-1994, the unofficial parallel market rate depreciated to YR 103 per US dollar.

In early 1995, the main official exchange rate was devalued to YR 50 (from YR 12) while the free market rate depreciated further to around YR 125. This led to sharp real exchange depreciation. To limit the depreciation of the free market rate the CBY form time-to-time suspended the operations of moneychangers, pushing foreign exchange transactions in the parallel market underground.

In January 1996, the authorities began a two-staged process of unification and liberalization of the foreign exchange market. In the first stage, the official exchange rate was devalued from YR 50 to YR 100 per US dollar and all other official rates were eliminated. This rate continued to apply only to budget accounting, customs valuations and transactions, the CBY and the Ministry of Finance. After a short period under a dual rate system, full exchange market unification was implemented in July 1996, and an independently floating exchange rate regime was adopted. All government and CBY transactions, including customs valuations, began to use the unified market

---

[73]   This section draws heavily on IMF (2001).

rate thus completing the second liberalization stage in August 1996. Finally, in December 1996, Yemen formally accepted the obligations under Article VIII (sections 2, 3 and 4) of the Fund's Articles of Agreements, and since then has maintained an exchange system free of exchange restrictions on current or capital account transactions. Again the nominal depreciation that occurred at the time of the unification of the exchange rates led to a sharp depreciation to the REER.

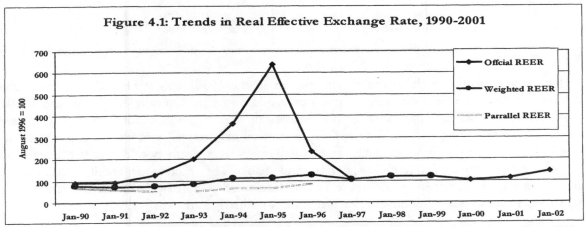

Source: Data obtained from the Middle East Department of the International Monetary Fund in May 2002.

With the authorities move to a floating exchange rate system throughout the second half of the 1990s (Figure 4.1), the Rial broadly stabilized in real effective terms, some small appreciation in real terms between end-1996 and end-1999 partly reflected a reluctance to tolerate substantial variability in the exchange rate. Through interest rate policy, moral suasion, and the regular auctioning of foreign exchange to moneychangers and banks, the CBY attempted to stabilize the exchange rate in times of turmoil. In part, interventions reflected also an attempt to smooth sharp seasonal peaks in demand for foreign exchange (specially around the Ramadan and Hajj seasons), given the limited depth of the private market. For example, in 1998 the CBY employed its limited monetary tools to ease the pressure on the exchange rate. It raised the official benchmark interest rate (up to 3.5 % in real terms) and removed remuneration on foreign currency deposits at the CBY and spent half of its reserves to limit exchange rate depreciation during 1998 to7% against the US dollar. In 1999 and 2001, the authorities allowed a faster rate of depreciation coupled with further interest rate tightening. The REER has remained at the same level during 1998-2001.

CONSTANT MARKET SHARE ANALYSIS (CMSA)

While Yemen's export performance in the late 1990s has been very good, manufacturing exports have been stagnant. What factors have driven successful total export performance on one hand and stagnant manufacturing exports on the other hand and what policies were behind them? To address this question, the constant market share analysis (CMSA) was undertaken. It decomposes trade growth into three factors: (i) world trade effect representing the growth in Yemeni exports due to the growth of world imports: (ii) composition effect (demand structure effect) which measures the changes in Yemen' exports due to the fact that world consumption for the various products exported by Yemen is growing at a different rate, and (iii) competitiveness effect representing the growth of Yemen' exports due to a change in Yemen's market share. CMSA is applied to Yemen's manufactured, oil and total merchandise exports (Table 4.3).

TABLE 4.3: YEMEN: CONSTANT MARKET SHARE ANALYSIS (%)

	Manufactured Exports		Non-Oil Exports		Total Exports	
	1991-1994	1994-1999	1991-1994	1994-1999	1991-1994	1994-1999
World Trade Effect	214.8	97.1	35.5	5.0	81.8	80.9
Composition Effect	26.6	4.2	-0.7	-2.0	-10.7.6	-27.3
Competitiveness	-141.4	-1.3	65.2	96.9	125.8	46.5
Total	100	100	100	100	100	100

Source: Someya (2001).

For total exports, much of the export growth in the 1990s was attributed to world trade effect. Competitiveness effect was strong and positive although it deteriorated in the late 1990s. However, the compositional effect was negative suggesting that Yemen's export structure has gone against the structural change in world demand. For non-oil exports, 97% of export growth can be attributed to improved competitiveness with small assistance from world market expansion (particularly for commodities such as coffee and fish). The picture is totally different in manufacturing exports whereas world trade effect dominated 97% of growth in the late 1990s. Competitiveness effect was behind poor performance particularly in the early 1990s.

BOX 4.2: YEMEN' EXPORTS OF MANUFACTURED GOODS

Yemen's manufacturing exports reached US$ 23 million in 2000. The country's manufacturing export ratio (1.1% of total merchandise exports) is the second lowest among 230 countries in the world, only next to Iraq. The low level of manufacturing exports is not commensurate with the level of manufacturing output in domestic production (7.5% of GDP in 2000). In addition to their small size, Yemen's manufacturing exports have been stagnant in the late 1990s. The average real export growth rate from 1996 to 2000 was −1.4% compared with 6.8% for world manufacturing export, and 2.1% for the 41 low-income countries.

Yemen's trade partners in manufactured exports are OECD, South Asia and East Africa (accounting for more than 90% of manufacturing exports). In terms of individual countries, India, UK and Ethiopia are the steady trade partners in manufacturing exports. The linkage with neighboring countries has been very weak indicating that Yemen is not benefiting from geographical agglomeration effect in manufacturing industry. The main manufacturing exports are petroleum products, household cleaning products, beverages and tobacco products, textile and leather machinery, non-electric parts and appliances.

Someya (2001) attempted to investigate: (i) if Yemen's manufacturing capability is fully exploited? and (ii) why the share of manufactured exports in total exports lagged behind the share of manufacturing value-added into total GDP? Accordingly, the optimum level of manufacturing production and export were estimated by running two cross-sectional regressions with dependent variables (manufacturing exports and manufacturing value-added) against Gross National Income per capita, tertiary enrollment ratios, population, squared urban population to total population ratios and foreign direct investment using data for 1998. The regression results show that all the variables are statistically significant and that the size of coefficients of tertiary education and FDI (0.86 and 0.33) in manufacturing output, respectively, much larger than the corresponding figures (0.43 and 0.06) for manufacturing exports. This indicates that policies relevant to tertiary education and FDI liberalization are very effective in promoting manufacturing exports. The variables are robust and consistently demonstrate statistical significance in different formulation.

Using the formula estimated in the regression analysis above, the optimum level of manufacturing exports as well as manufacturing value added are simulated. Simulated optimum level of manufacturing values added is US$ 860 million while actual value is US$ 773 million. The corresponding figure for manufacturing export is US$ 139 million far greater than actual value, US$ 23 million. Then, the manufacturing capacity utilization rates are calculated by dividing actual figures by estimated optimum level. While 90% of manufacturing production capability is utilized, only 17% of export capability is utilized. Thus, Yemen's manufacturing export capacity has not been fully exploited.

Reforms of the foreign exchange regime implemented during 1991-1996 and trade liberalization measures adopted since early 1990s were the two most important factors behind improved competitiveness of Yemen exports.[74] All foreign exchange restrictions on the current account transactions were removed and the exchange rate was floated in 1996. This resulted in amelioration in price competitiveness of commodity exports because the real effective exchange rate (REER) of the Rial improved considerably creating a congenial environment for export boom in the late 1990s (Figure 4.1). Trade liberalization policies also played an important role in improved competitiveness.[75] In 1991, the 100% import deposit requirement was abolished and the positive list was replaced by a negative list in 1993. A comprehensive reform of the tariff and trade system was initiated in 1996.[76] The maximum tariff was reduced to 25%, and the tariff rate for imported inputs was reduced to 5%. In 1998, non-tariff barriers such as import bans were tarifficated or removed. Currently, Yemen is one of the most trade-liberalized countries in the MENA region. Its ratio of tax revenues on international trade to total imports as a proxy for a nominal effective mean tariff is 5.2%, far lower than MENA' reformers such as Jordan (6.5%), Tunisia (5.9%), and Egypt (12.2%).

Why did improvement in international competitiveness boosted commodity exports but not manufacturing exports? One reason lies in the competitive edge. The quality of the commodities such as coffee is not very much different by location of production and, thus, the price competitiveness is often a unique edge in international markets. However, price is not a unique edge for competitiveness in manufacturing products. Quality is often more important than price effects. Another possible reason is gestation period, i.e., the time-lag after which reduced priced inputs penetrate into manufacturing production and production efficiency starts to improve. Liberalization of foreign exchange transactions and other trade liberalization measures benefited both manufacturing and non-manufacturing exports by drastically reducing imports prices and facilitating access to international markets for cheap intermediate and capital goods. In fact, capital goods imports, which were falling even in nominal terms in the first half of the 1990s, jumped up with nominal growth rate, 39.3% and 58.9% in 1996 and 1997 while the corresponding figures of the world import were rather moderate, 5.8% and 6.3%, respectively. Table 4.4 below shows that after trade liberalization there was a surge in consumer goods (food, beverages and tobacco, *etc.*). There was also a rapid increase in capital goods, particularly, machinery and transport equipment

However, availability of capital goods does not necessarily lead to efficiency improvements, which require many other inputs such as human resources. In fact, subsequent to trade and exchange liberalization, manufacturing intermediate goods imports did not increase as much as imports of capital goods. Imports of raw material, chemicals, minerals and lubricants and other animal and vegetable oils did not witness significant increases. This may be why competitiveness in commodity export improved after adoption of the floating exchange regime in 1996 while that in manufacturing exports did not as we have seen from the CMSA.

---

[74]   Upon the unification in 1990, there existed multi-exchange systems as well as many restrictions on foreign exchange transactions in Yemen.

[75]   Before reforms, there was a positive list on imports and almost all the imports required licenses or official permission from government agencies. In addition, imports were also subject to a customs duty under a tariff structure, which was constituted of 15 bands with tariff rates ranging from 5 to 200%. Moreover, the 100% import deposit was required to the commercial banks to obtain letters of credit for imports.

[76]   Under the reformed tariff structure, the mean tariff was reduced from 27% to 12%.

TABLE 4.4: TREND AND COMPOSITION OF YEMEN'S IMPORTS, 1994-2000

	1994	1995	1996	1997	1998	1999	2000
Food and live animals	**450.3**	**542.8**	**941.3**	**802.0**	**776.2**	**663.9**	**687.2**
Meat and live animals	70.9	48.8	39.5	48.8	80.0	83.3	89.3
Dairy products and eggs	50.3	36.2	61.3	75.3	83.9	71.3	86.4
Cereals and their products	198.5	315.2	648.7	445.9	414.5	338.8	312.8
Vegetables and fruits	29.4	26.8	40.0	41.0	50.5	41.3	51.4
Sugar and its products, and honey	59.1	80.1	111.9	137.4	98.6	93.9	107.9
Coffee, tea, and spices	20.7	20.5	19.1	18.3	18.2	16.3	13.6
Other	21.3	15.2	20.8	35.3	30.5	19.1	25.7
Beverages and Tobacco	**32.7**	**32.4**	**33.2**	**35.8**	**43.6**	**40.5**	**38.9**
Raw materials	**41.4**	**43.8**	**45.4**	**51.7**	**48.6**	**42.3**	**50.6**
Oilseeds	7.1	4.3	7.1	15.5	11.4	10.4	11.6
Wood and cork	26.7	30.4	26.0	24.7	26.7	22.0	27.7
Other	7.6	9.2	12.3	11.5	10.5	9.9	11.3
Minerals, fuels, and lubricants	**236.3**	**121.3**	**165.8**	**223.4**	**139.4**	**161.6**	**277.8**
Animal and vegetable oils	**26.4**	**66.7**	**50.8**	**73.1**	**83**	**67.0**	**90.3**
Chemicals	**107.8**	**126.3**	**136.2**	**166.5**	**211.1**	**187.0**	**225.1**
Manufactured goods, classified by materials	**296.3**	**353.3**	**298.8**	**353.1**	**374.9**	**307.2**	**341.2**
Rubber manufactures	28.9	32.9	32.5	38.3	33.5	26.8	28.4
Wood and cork	14.0	11.4	10.5	16.4	18.6	8.2	12.1
Paper manufactures	27.6	42.3	34.6	34.5	48.6	43.9	54.3
Textiles	33.6	37.2	33.8	37.2	38.1	35.2	33.3
Nonmetallic mineral manufactures	39.0	39.7	45.7	44.4	44.1	38.1	47.7
Iron and steel	96.7	117.1	83.0	107.0	115.8	96.2	100.1
Metal manufactures	34.0	52.4	40.8	48.9	48.4	36.5	41.9
Other	22.5	20.3	17.8	26.4	27.8	22.3	23.4
Machinery and transport equipment	**285.5**	**355.2**	**373.1**	**424.9**	**525.1**	**431.8**	**484.3**
Machinery	192.9	245.3	244.1	316.7	396.6	105.8	87.8
Road vehicles	87.1	101.8	120.7	103.0	106.5	96.0	173.6
Other transport equipment	5.5	8.1	8.3	5.3	22	8.4	7.8
Other	0.0	0.0	0.0	0	0	221.6	215.2
Miscellaneous manufactured articles	**80.0**	**96.7**	**83.8**	**96.9**	**114.4**	**106.1**	**104.4**
Furniture	3.7	7.4	8.5	6.8	8.6	8.3	8.2
Clothing and footwear	36.2	32.2	23.37	30.6	37.19	25.6	27.2
Professional and scientific instruments	9.4	8.2	9.4	12.8	24.1	36.3	26.4
Other	30.7	48.9	42.6	46.7	44.6	35.9	42.6
Other commodities	0.1	0.4	1.0	4.4	11.3	1.0	24.0
Total imports, c.i.f.	**1,556.9**	**1,739.0**	**2,129.4**	**2,231.8**	**2,327.6**	**2,008.3**	**2,323.9**

Source: Data between 1994-1998 are IMF estimates and data for 1999 and 2000 are from CSO converted using average exchange rate.

REVEALED COMPARATIVE ADVANTAGE (RCA) ANALYSIS

Aggregated macro-analysis shows that Yemen generally demonstrated a good performance in commodity exports while manufacturing exports were stagnant in the late 1990s even after exchange rate regime and trade reforms. For this purpose, RCA was calculated for detailed export items.[77] RCA was calculated at two levels, one against world export and another against GCC and East Africa.[78]

Yemen did not have many commodities that are comparatively advantageous in the international market while Yemen improved its competitiveness in many items and even in manufacturing products in neighboring markets. Yemen's RCA against the world export shows that there are only 10 commodities (9 commodities in 1995) which have RCA greater than unity in 2000

---

[77] $RCAij = (Xij/X.j)/(Xi./X..)$: RCAij is Revealed comparative advantage of industry i in country j, Xij: export of industry i in country j, X.j: total export in country j, Xi.: world export in industry i and X..: world total export.

[78] GCC includes Bahrain, Kuwait, Oman, Qatar, Saudi Arabia and UAE. East Africa includes Djibouti, Eritrea, Ethiopia, Somali and Sudan.

(Table 4.5). In terms of improved RCA, Yemen has three export items with improved RCA between 1995 and 2000 (live animals, animals for pets and coins) in addition to the three products that did not have export data in 1995 (fish, margarine, and silver and platinum ores). It should be noted that: (i) oil export and coffee aggravated RCA from 1995 to 2000 and (ii) Yemen did not have any manufacturing items which have RCA greater than unity.

TABLE 4.5: REVEALED COMPARATIVE ADVANTAGE (RCA) AGAINST THE WORLD

	SITC Code	RCA Greater than 1.0			RCA Growth	
		1991	1995	2000	1991-1995	1995-2000
Live animals	001		2.02	2.80		0.78
Fish (fresh and simply preserved)	031	1.07		2.57		
Rice	042		1.10			
Coffee	071	3.13	3.0	2.14	-0.13	-0.86
Margarine and shortening	091			2.39		
Hides and skins (exc. Fur skins)	211	3.67	3.46	2.04	-0.31	-1.42
Nonferrous metal scrap	284		1.75			
Silver and Platinum ores	285			2.01		
Petroleum (crude and partly refined)	331	13.78	19.03	12.58	5.25	-6.45
Petroleum products	332	5.32	6.59	5.16	1.27	-1.43
Leather	611	1.13				
Animals, for pets and zoo	941		1.35	1.89		0.54
Coins- other than gold, not legal tender	961		2.87	4.41		1.54

Source: Someya (2001).

The picture is better in RCA analysis against the GCC and East African countries than that against total world exports. The number of items, which have RCA greater than unity, increases from 18 in 1995 to 27 in 2000. Out of 27 products, five products even improved RCA such as live animals, raw fish, maize, dried fruits, and coins. In addition, 17 products, which had no export in 1995, became competitive with RCA greater than unity in 2000. Apart from the above-mentioned items, major items, which have high RCA, are fresh fruits and nuts, fresh or dried vegetables, margarine and shortening, tobacco products, and silver and platinum ores [Someya (2001)]. There are many products which grew rapidly in the late 1990s such as footwear, travel goods, handbags and similar articles, wood and cork manufactures (excluding furniture and non-manufactured textile fibers), and waste. However, world market grew much faster than Yemen's export in those items. As a result, Yemen's RCA for those items are not greater than unity.

MARKET POSITIONING (RISING AND FALLING STARS)[79]

Has Yemen been taking the right market strategy? Or, has Yemen been operating in expanding markets or contracting markets? As we have seen in CMSA, Yemen's export composition had a negative impact on Yemen's export growth in the late 1990s. For that purpose, Yemen's market positioning analysis is undertaken (Figure 4.2). Those products classified under Rising Stars in year 2000 account for 61.5% of total non-oil exports, which accounted only 6.6% in 1995. This

---

[79] Rising Stars includes those products in which both Yemen as well as world exports increased over the period. Falling Stars includes those products in which Yemeni export increased while world decreased. Missing Opportunity includes those products in which Yemeni export decreased while world export increased. Retreat includes those products in which both Yemeni and world exports decreased.

figure is very high even compared with other middle-income countries. The corresponding figures for Tunisia, Morocco, Jordan, Egypt and Chile are 41%, 30%, 16%, 19% and 9% during 1990-1998.

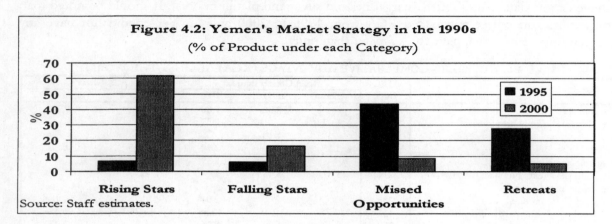

Figure 4.2: Yemen's Market Strategy in the 1990s
(% of Product under each Category)

Source: Staff estimates.

In terms of products, a considerable number of products categorized under Rising Stars are actually manufacturing sectors. In fact, out of 53 products classified under Rising Stars, 47 products are manufacturing products. This indicates that Yemen has been expanding exports in the international markets that have also been expanding for the same period. Therefore, Yemen exports are competitive in regional markets, Yemen has been operating in expanding international markets and Yemen's industrial composition is better than other MENA countries.

PART III:

TAPPING THE POTENTIALS OF YEMEN'S ECONOMY

CHAPTER 5:
HIGH AND SUSTAINED GDP GROWTH IN YEMEN: THE WAY FORWARD

High and sustained rate of economic growth in Yemen is a necessary, though not sufficient, condition for reduction of high incidence of poverty (estimated at more than 40% in 1998) and raising the living standards of the Yemeni citizens, particularly given the prevailing high population growth rates (estimated by the GoY at 3.5% and by the Bank at 2.7%). The current plans and strategies of the GoY (the Strategy Vision 2025, the SFYP, the I-PRSP and the PRSP) recognize the importance of economic growth to meet the socio-economic development goals and for effective poverty reduction in Yemen.

The necessary conditions for rapid economic growth are now better in Yemen than they were at any time in the past. Yemen is endowed with rich natural resources (fisheries, gas, oil and mineral reserves, fertile land, *etc.*); the country has a strategic location and natural endowments for services (e.g., trade, transport and tourism); young and dynamic labor force with abundance of entrepreneurial skills. In addition, Yemen currently enjoys political stability, macroeconomic stability, and improved foreign relations. It also built democratic institutions and created an open trade regime. Furthermore, the GoY embarked since mid-1990s on implementation of stabilization and structural reform programs and has since then made good progress on both fronts.

Nonetheless, achieving high and sustained GDP growth rates in the short- and long-terms is still a daunting challenge. Evidence in this Report suggests that the main obstacle to rapid and sustained economic growth is the ***weak governance*** that characterizes Yemen in addition to the weaknesses in domestic security, property rights and rule of law systems. Weak governance in Yemen is manifested by widespread corruption, lack of transparency and accountability, inefficiency in the interaction of public officials and private business, ineffective or absent market promoting institutions such as those enforcing contracts (courts, tribunals, *etc.*), poor performance of the public sector in terms of delivering essential goods and implementing programs, associated lack of incentives and skills in the civil service, weak enforceability of contracts and rulings.

In addition to putting in order the governance situation, there are areas that should receive government priority in the short and medium terms including: (i) enhancing domestic security to boost economic activity in all economic sectors, and particularly the "promising" sectors such as tourism, mining and extractive industries, as well as attracting FDI; both are currently hampered by the security conditions; (ii) removing excessive and arbitrary regulations to strengthen basic infrastructure and other services and to attract private investment into these sectors; (iii) reform of the legal and judicial systems and strengthening the enforcement of rulings and clarification of property rights and resolution of conflicts over land ownership; and (iv) sustained implementation of civil service reforms to improve delivery of public services. In terms of sequencing of reforms, it is important again to give higher priority to putting into place governance structures before embarking on other reforms. It will be extremely difficult for Yemen to build market-promoting institutions, such as well-functioning judiciary, before to addressing governance problems because the impact of a well-functioning judiciary in an environment where overall governance is weak is likely to be negligible. Improving the domestic security situation should be the second highest priority.

Given the strong emphasis on the private sector for meeting the economic targets of the SFYP and the Vision 2025, a private sector survey was conducted for this study. Based on firm's perceptions as well as their actual experience, there are five main areas of impediments to growth and productivity: (i) poor governance especially corruption; (ii) lack of security and rule of law (violence, smuggling and lengthy dispute settlement); (iii) macroeconomic and policy instability; (iv) problems with tax rates and administration and (v) inadequate infrastructure especially electricity services.

Good governance in Yemen would be ensured if the GoY put in place mechanisms and measures to ensure efficient allocation of public resources, effective provision of public services, accountability, transparency and minimal corruption. Among the many areas in which action is needed, three are paramount: enhanced accountability of the government and the civil service, better legal and contract-enforcement systems, and reduced regulatory barriers. Strengthening the accountability of the public sector in its role in regulating private activity would require extensive civil service reform and administrative accountability measures, some of which have already been initiated by the government. Reduction in the number of civil servants overseeing the private sector, and clarification of their roles and responsibilities, is a clear need. At the same time, there is a need for increased administrative accountability mechanisms, including procurement reform and better auditing and oversight. Better formal legal and contract-enforcement systems are needed to reduce the high cost and uncertainty associated with informal dispute resolution in Yemen. In terms of legislation, new laws, particularly modern commercial codes, will be required as part of the development of a workable legal system and to support a market based economy. Specific areas include the financial sector (secured transactions and real and personal property registers), insolvency, bankruptcy and others. Private sector firms tend to face burdensome regulatory and administrative hurdles procedures in setting up businesses, and in commencing/expanding business operations. Thus, improved coordination among government agencies, perhaps aided by the elimination of investment licensing, is an important step towards the development of private sector activity. Another way to achieve this is to create a 'one stop' or 'first stop' shop for potential entrepreneurs and business owners (such as the GIA). Formal complaint and appeals procedures attached to this regulatory administration would also provide a mechanism for the transmission of vital information and feedback about the impact of government policies.

There are three levels of uncertainty for firms in Yemen: uncertainty about the macro-fiscal environment, uncertainty about the course and sequence of structural policies, and uncertainty due to the lack of market information. Separate sets of practices will need to be adopted to address each of these. What is needed at the macroeconomic level is to continue Yemen's concentrated and sustained effort toward prudent macroeconomic management, promoting open trade policies and a competitive exchange rate. This would be especially important in times of lower oil prices. A more transparent, inclusive and open policymaking process can reduce structural policy uncertainty, in turn. Reducing such firm-specific uncertainties would require a range of institution-building, and the need to make available planning and business resources to the firms.

To tap on the big potentials of Yemen's economic sectors, there are also a few but daunting policy obstacles that confront all sectors as well specific problems to individual sectors. Poor access to infrastructure (including electricity and transportation), insecurity, and weakness in the financial system are among the most important barriers. Therefore, promoting greater competition and efficiency in these areas would facilitate economic growth. The following Matrix provides a list of recommended policy reforms and measures needed in the various economic sectors in the light of the findings of the previous chapters. While the list of suggested reforms and measures is quite long and its full implementation may not be feasible in the short and medium terms, the Matrix singled priory reforms that warrant immediate government attention and their pursuit should precede all other suggested reforms.

Fortunately, the GoY recognizes also the importance of the suggested key reforms and has already embarked on addressing some of them. However, given the nature of the existing constraints, the envisaged reforms are expected to take longer time and would require strong political commitment and systematic and persistent purist of reforms in the short- and long-terms.

Plan of Action for Reduction of Constraints in Economic Sectors

Main Objective: Ensuring a High and Sustained GDP Growth for Sustained Poverty Reduction

Major Potentials	Major Constraints	SYFP Objectives	Observation & Comments	Proposed Policies and Reform Measures	Priority Reforms
1. Agricultural Sector:					
(i) huge fishery resources *(see 2.1 below)*; (ii) suitable weather for many crops; (iii) one third of cultivable land is currently unutilized; (iv) good export potentials due to proximity to the Gulf markets; (v) huge potential for increasing productivity from cultivated area given current low yields for most crops in most areas; (vi) world famous varieties of crops (e.g, Arabica coffee).	(i) substantial yield gap (up to 60% for some crops); (ii) limited water resources; (iii) half of cultivated area is rainfed and vulnerable to shortfalls in rainfall; (iv) limited arable land for cultivation exacerbated by deforestation, desertification and fragmentation of holdings; (v) increased plantation of Qat; (vi) high population growth and rapid urbanization; (vii) prevalence of traditional cultivation methods; (viii) high post-harvest losses; and, (ix) agricultural exports are hampered by high prices on niche markets and lack of quality control.	The plan targets an annual growth rate of 6.7% during 2001-2005, to ensure food security. The Plan also aims to increase agricultural exports, farmers' income and reduce underemployment in the sector.	The SFYP growth target for agricultural value-added seems high by historical trends and the experience of other countries mainly because of high target for fisheries sub-sector. Targets for non-fisheries agricultural output of 6.1% can be achieved if the constraints in the sector are removed, non-Qat cultivated areas and yields are increased, Qat plantation is controlled, and irrigation management is improved.	(i) increase irrigation efficiency from the current 40% rate; (ii) enhance non-farm activities and rain-fed crops; (iii) develop water resources and improve water recovery techniques, recharging underground water basins, resort to water harvesting techniques that are economically feasible; (iv) construct more small water dams, dikes and canals to improve the efficiency and conservation of water; (v) accelerate development in the coastal areas to encourage relocation of population from areas with low water resources; (vi) improve agricultural and veterinary extension services and their coverage (e.g., seed varieties, and fertilization techniques,) to ensure increase in agricultural productivity; (vii) reduce post-harvest losses; and, (viii) promote terrace rehabilitation and improve watershed and range management.	Change the incentive structure resulting from price distortions (e.g, low cost of water abstraction due to diesel subsidy and low tariffs for electricity).
1.1. Fisheries Sub-Sector:					
(i) Fish reserves are estimated at 850,000 tons; (ii) warm waters throughout the year; (iii) considerable demersal and pelagic fish resources; (iv) high value fish stocks (rock lobster, cuttlefish, shrimp and bottom-dwelling species); and, (v) there is scope for fish production from aquaculture and mari-culture.	(i) limited infrastructure (landing centers, jetties, ice plants, chill rooms, and auction sites) and basic services accessible to fishermen; (ii) lack of basic data, statistics and information on resources in the fisheries sector; (iii) inefficiency in the management of fisheries and marine life; (iv) incomplete legislation, regulations to regulate coastal and commercial fishing, which expose the fish wealth to overexploitation and illegitimate fishing; (v) lack of quality controls in the fishing activities; (vi) current licensing is not based on reliable statistics of standing stocks; and, (vii) poor performance of institutions.	SFYP considers fisheries as potential and promising sector for achieving high GDP growth and targets an average annual 13% growth in its output during 2001-2005. Annual output is targeted to increase from 135,000 tons in 2000 to 248,000 and the sector's contribution to GDP is planned to increase from 1% in 2000 to 1.6% by 2005.	The objectives appear realistic, provided that they will be reached by an increase in prices through improved quality and marketing mechanisms and reduction of un-controlled production rather than only increases in volume of landing. A stock assessment and a utilization plan are high priority.	(i) improve fisheries resource management and development of small scale fisheries; (ii) enhance fish marketing and strengthen export marketing networks; (iii) improve the performance of the institutions and research centers in developing modern breeding and culture farms; (iv) improve management, control and evaluation of fishing activities, their proper exploitation, and protection from pollution and over-exploitation; (v) remove constraints to private sector provision of basic infrastructure and facilities (e.g, refrigeration, storage, transportation); (vi) revise legislation, procedures, and regulations related to traditional and commercial fishing; (vii) establish quality control laboratories in the main ports and fishing centers to ensure international quality standards; and (viii) improve capacities of the Coast Guards in marine control and inspection to prevent foreign piracy and to halt overexploitation and pollution.	Undertake a stock evaluation study and assess the feasibility of current licensing schemes in the light of the study.
2. Industrial Sector:					
(i) potentials for new oil and gas discoveries; (ii) large mining potentials; (iii) potentials in manufacturing activities (e.g, garment) given availability of natural resources, cheap and abundant manpower, and accessibility to regional and	(i) financing constraints to tap gas resources; (ii) poor incentive framework and weak institutions hamper manufacturing activities; (iii) security situation deters mining activities; (iv) weak infrastructure and high production costs; and, (iv) weak legal and judicial systems do not encourage industrial	SFYP aims to increase industrial activities by 3.0% on average between 2001-2005.	The target set by the SFYP for growth in industrial value added is very low although it masks very high growth rates planned for some sub-sectors (manufacturing construction and water and electricity). The predicted stagnation in real value added of the oil sector is an underestimation of	Main reforms to tap the potentials in this sector are outlined below.	See sections below

Major Potentials	Major Constraints	SYFP Objectives	Observation & Comments	Proposed Policies and Reform Measures	Priority Reforms
international markets.	activities.		recent discoveries.		

2.1. Oil Sector:

Major Potentials	Major Constraints	SYFP Objectives	Observation & Comments	Proposed Policies and Reform Measures	Priority Reforms
Currently, proven reserves are estimated at about 2.8 billion barrels. However, prospects for new discoveries are promising particularly after signing the Border agreement with Saudi Arabia. The country has still unexploited territory and future technologies may permit utilization of currently inaccessible reserves of oil and gas.	(i) difficulties in making projection on oil production from both existing fields and newer ones; (ii) high volatility in oil prices particularly after the events of September 11th; (iii) lack of domestic capacities for surveys and exploration; (iv) dominance of foreign oil companies in exploration and production; (v) security concerns impact production levels, the pipelines, and detract foreign companies from investing in the oil sector in Yemen; and, (vi) market concentration in oil exports to emerging Asian countries.	The SFYP assumes that oil value-added will be stagnant during the plan as a result of expected decline in production from producing fields (2.5% annually), additional production from new discoveries (12.5% of 2000 levels annually) and oil prices at US$ 18-22 per barrel.	(i) SFYP's projections need to be revised in the light of new information on oil production as well as the outlook for oil prices; (ii) with expected high volatility of oil prices and decline in oil production levels, oil revenues need to be saved or invested gradually in long-term high-return activities, and (iii) the expected decline in oil value-added will affect incomes negatively but may also have some positive effects on substitution to non oil activities (due to low oil prices and reduced Dutch disease);	(i) expand exploration work to cover all regions of Yemen and coastal areas, especially after signing the Border agreement with Saudi Arabia; (ii) enhance oversight, regulatory and control capabilities in the management and production of oil; (iii) encourage the local private sector to invest in the sector particularly in service provision to the oil fields; (iv) develop and improve the capacities for marketing oil in the external markets; (v) ration local demand for oil products and improve the efficiency of their use by eliminating the subsidies; and (vi) promote the establishment of industries that rely on oil derivative products as primary or intermediary inputs with a view towards increasing the economic benefit and achieving economic savings with the other sectors such as manufacturing.	Review production-sharing agreements in the light of past experience and experience of other countries to increase the attractiveness of investment in the oil sector and to attract foreign companies.

2.2. Gas:

Major Potentials	Major Constraints	SYFP Objectives	Observation & Comments	Proposed Policies and Reform Measures	Priority Reforms
Gas proven reserves are estimated at 12 – 15 billion cubic feet.	(i) competition from MENA countries with developed infrastructure (e.g., Qatar and Oman); (ii) Gas Export project requires large financial resources (about US$ 5 billion); and, (iii) lack of secured markets for the sale of gas.	The SFYP aims to secure financial resources for the Gas Export Project, increase domestic gas consumption in electricity generation and industry.	Given the existing constraints, it is unlikely that the gas sub-sector will have a tangible impact on economic growth during the implementation of the SFYP.	(i) encourage power stations, factories, production units and motor vehicles to convert from the use of diesel and heavy fuels to the use of natural gas instead.	Intensify efforts to promote and market natural gas and review current arrangements

2.3. Mining:

Major Potentials	Major Constraints	SYFP Objectives	Observation & Comments	Proposed Policies and Reform Measures	Priority Reforms
Promising reserves of gold, platinum, titanium and other mineral reserves (e.g., gypsum, marble, basalt, etc.). Many territories are yet to be explored.	(i) disputes in property rights and ambiguity of laws and regulations organizing land ownership and utilization of natural resources; (ii) poor transportation network to link potential productive areas to seaports and other outlets, in addition to high cost of transportation; (iii) security concerns and tribal conflicts over land and resources, and (iv) weak promotion activities to attract FDI into mining activities.	SFYP aims to increase the share of mining to 0.1% of GDP, to enhance its contribution in the development of the regions where minerals are discovered and in the creation of more jobs. The plan targets an annual rate of growth of mining of 10%.	The plan targets are unlikely to be met unless concerted efforts are exerted to remove the identified constraints that hamper mining activities such as security concerns, transport networks, and clarification of property rights and land issues.	(i) complete geological surveys, mining maps and assessments of mineral reserves and the potential for commercial exploitation of the minerals and mineral ores; (ii) upgrade the legislative and institutional framework for regulating the exploration and exploitation of industrial and construction minerals and resources; (iii) prepare the essential basic infrastructure, especially in the areas of promising reserves of mineral resources, with a view towards improving their extraction, exploitation and transport domestically and to overseas markets; and (iv) implement an intensive promotional program on the investment opportunities in the mining sector.	Enhance domestic security (e.g., Marib and Al-Jouf governorates).

2.4. Water and Electricity:

Major Potentials	Major Constraints	SYFP Objectives	Observation & Comments	Proposed Policies and Reform Measures	Priority Reforms
There are enormous gas potentials that can be used in electricity generation by conversion of stations to gas turbines.	(i) huge energy losses (38% in 2000); (ii) weak administrative and financial capacities in the sector; (iii) high cost of operations and inability to collect enough revenues; and (iv) rural electrification is difficult because of dispersion of population in smaller communities.	SFYP aims to raise output of the sector by 7.5% per annum. It plans to raise the electricity coverage to 40%, and reduce losses to 33%. It also plans raising water supply for households use by 9.5% annually.	These sectoral targets depend largely on government investments because activities are mainly driven by the public sector. Private sector involvement in generation, supply and distribution of water and electricity will facilitate the realization of the plan targets.	(i) attract private sector investments into power generation and distribution as well as water supply; (ii) give more attention to rehabilitation of existing networks; (iii) introduce cost recovery in water supply; (iv) give high priority to densely populated areas in rural electrification; and, (v) strengthen administrative and financial capacities of public authorities to ensure their future sustainability.	Reform of PEC to ensure its financial sustainability and review tariffs for public utilities.

Major Potentials	Major Constraints	SYFP Objectives	Observation & Comments	Proposed Policies and Reform Measures	Priority Reforms
2.5. Manufacturing:					
(i) abundance of the raw materials (agricultural products, fruits, fish, minerals); (ii) large population compared with other Gulf countries; (iii) availability of labor with low cost; (iv) strategic transit location between South East Asia and Europe, the Gulf and the Horn of Africa; (v) the establishment of Aden Free Zone (with the necessary infrastructures).	(i) high production costs due to poor infrastructure (e.g., electricity supply, water and sewerage) and high cost of transportation due to weak networks, poor roads, and monopolies in the sector; (ii) low productivity for low technical and professional caliber; (iii) dumping and smuggling and unfair competition; (iv) weak legislative, judicial, administrative and enforcement systems; (v) security concerns; (vi) low level of domestic demand; (vii) lack of skilled manpower and high cost of foreign skilled workers; (viii) difficult access to credit, lack of term financing and high interest changes; (ix) high taxes rates; and (x) hassle by government bureaucrats.	The plan targets an average annual rate of growth of manufacturing value-added of more than 9% (10% for non-refining manufacturing and 7.5% for oil refining). It aims to increase the share of the manufacturing sector in the GDP from 7.5% in 2000 to 8.8% 2005. The plan also seeks to encourage and give incentives to promising export manufacturers, and to support the development of small-scale and traditional handicraft industries to create job opportunities and to alleviate poverty.	The realization of these targets largely depends on government removal of the constraints in the sector, further trade liberalization, improvements in infrastructure and utilities, improvements in the legal and judicial systems. There are good prospects for manufacturing of food and tobacco for exports to the GCC and African countries. There are also good prospects for manufacturing of textiles and garments, construction materials, and furniture and wood work because of the comparative advantages of Yemen in such industry. The prospects of manufacturing are better with the development of the free zone in Aden. Finally, Yemen has not yet utilized its capacity for exports of manufacturers.	(i) assess the feasibility of establishing industrial zones with basic services and facilities; (ii) alter the incentive framework to encourage labor-intensive industries (e.g., the investment law); (iii) review, streamline and simplify the laws and regulations related to industry activities; (iv) improve capacities for monitoring and implementing industrial standards and controls to ensure quality improvements and to protect consumers; (v) simplify export procedures; remove administrative constraints and improve the incentive framework facing exporters; (vi) assist small industries and the handicraft enterprises by training programs, promotion and marketing their products and easy access to credit (vii) reorient the outcomes of the education system to the demand of the private sector for specializations, skills and qualifications as well as increase coordination between manufactures and local vocational training institutes; (viii) attract and encourage FDI and encourage joint investments opportunities to enhance technology transfers and to ease credit constraints; and (ix) enforce international standards and measures for consumer and environmental protection and raising the competitiveness of industries.	Improve basic infrastructure and essential utilities required for manufacturing (e.g., transportation and electricity);
2.6. Construction:					
(i) Good quality and relatively cheap building materials; (ii) high skills in construction and building; (iii) expanding manufacturing activities in construction materials.	(i) lack of regulations in property rights, land ownership, tenure, titles and registration as well as difficulties in enforcing laws and regulations;	SFYP targets average rise in construction value-added of 11% per annum and raising its contribution in GDP from 4.2% in 2000 to 5.5% by 2005.	Although there are good potentials and enormous needs for construction and buildings, achieving the plan targets appears challenging without addressing land and property rights issues.	Reform of the legal and judicial systems and strengthen the enforcement of their rules.	Formulate a comprehensive program to address land ownership, titles and registration.
3. Services Sector:					
Yemen has good potentials in tourism, and its location provides good prospects for trade and transport services. There is also wide scope for increasing the contribution of financial services in total GDP (banking and insurance).	(i) weak legal and judicial systems; (ii) despite liberalization and deregulation, monopolies in the sector deter private sector involvement; (iii) low financial system and low levels of financial intermediation; (iv) lack of technical skills for high quality services; and (v) security concerns in many governorates.	Services value-added is projected to increase by 8% per annum by the SFYP and to raise its contribution in GDP from 39% in 2000 to 43% by 2005.	The target growth rate of services seems rather ambitious and its attainment critically depends on a number of reforms in the business and investment environment	*See 3.1 to 3.4 below*	Improve regulatory environment for service delivery.
3.1. Tourism:					
(i) attractive uncontaminated natural environment and unique cultural heritage (historical cities of Sana'a, Shibam, and Zabid are part of UNESCO's World Cultural Heritage); (ii) 2,000 kms of coastline and more than 100	(i) structural impediments such as security concerns (kidnapping and proliferation of arms) and lack of necessary infrastructure; (ii) travel warnings to Yemen by many Western governments; (iii) lack of legal protection for investors and bureaucratic hurdles	(i) The SFYP targets an annual average growth rate of tourism (hotels and restaurants) at 11%; (ii) it also seeks to improve and modernize tourist facilities to create a more balanced,	(i) overall, the SFYP targets can be achieved if the constraints in the sector are removed; (ii) the targets for international tourism activities may be high given the existing constraints; average annual growth rate of tourism in the 1990s has been about 5% only;	(i) improve supporting infrastructure and related services; (ii) reassess air transport policies and facilitate access by foreign airlines to reduce air travel costs (liberalize landing rights, review landing fees, allow charter flights, and open more airports to international traffic); (iii) continue exhibitions of Yemen's cultural heritage	Improve travel security, particularly in tourism-designated areas and tackle the kidnapping

MAJOR POTENTIALS	MAJOR CONSTRAINTS	SYFP OBJECTIVES	OBSERVATION & COMMENTS	PROPOSED POLICIES AND REFORM MEASURES	PRIORITY REFORMS
islands (iii) outstanding and diversified landscapes with unique natural environment (e.g., Socotra island); (iv) mountains in the North, stone villages, and slopes sculpted by farmers, centuries ago, into spectacular terraces; (v) canyons in the South with green stretches of farmland surrounded by colored rocky walls and separated by deserted highlands; (vi) beautiful villages are nestled in the mountains facing dense palm grows; (viii) cities and villages are inhabited by traditional population whose lifestyle echoes centuries of civilization making Yemen an appealing destination for cultural and eco-tourism.	(frequent harassment by customs and tax officials, request of protection money in some urban areas); (iv) difficult and hostile investment environment (need of a local partner, difficult access to land, permits and utility connection); (v) high cost of hotel operations and air access reduce the margin of tour operators; (vi) public resources for tourism promotion are limited; (vii) inexperienced hotel management and staff results in poor services compared to prices; (viii) occupancy rates in beach destinations are negatively affected by seasonality determined by climatic factors; (ix) concerns of losing historical and cultural heritage and environmental degradation, and (x) cultural and religious values may inhibit some forms of leisure and beach tourism (gambling, alcohols, etc.).	profitable and economically efficient development of the accommodation capacity required to meet the future tourism demand.	(iii) the plan does not specify precise quantitative tourism development objectives over the next five years (though it indicate expected increase in the share of GDP).	and archeological treasures and combine them with well targeted and effective tourism promotion campaigns; (iv) create a positive investment climate for investment in general and tourism in particular; (v) raise awareness about the values of traditional architecture, handicraft activities, and life styles; (vi) establish effective environmental protection and cultural heritage preservation policies and laws and ensure that the agencies responsible for their enforcement, such as EPA, GOPHCY, GOAMM develop the managerial and technical capability to handle this task; (vii) foster the extension of the length of stay of international visitors by offering them the opportunity to combine their business visits with visits to sites of cultural, scenic and ecological interest (main motivation) or beach and resort areas (subsidiary product); and (viii) improve the returns of tourism by limiting foreign exchange leakages by increasing the national share of tourism investment and promoting the use of domestic inputs and materials, and national management and labor; all without compromising the quality of services.	incidents.

3.2. Transport and Communications:

MAJOR POTENTIALS	MAJOR CONSTRAINTS	SYFP OBJECTIVES	OBSERVATION & COMMENTS	PROPOSED POLICIES AND REFORM MEASURES	PRIORITY REFORMS
Yemen has advantageous location in the international shipping networks. A new container port was constructed in Aden and work is underway in three additional seaports. Yemen has also 14 airports (6 of which are international). Asphalt roads reached 6,586 km in 2000. There is scope for communication services (e.g., telephone coverage is now 2 lines for every 100 persons).	(i) technical specifications and standards for roads are not consistent and load limits are not enforced; (ii) lack of regular maintenance to roads; (iii) duplicity of agencies in land-transport sector; (iv) monopoly of transport offices (e.g., Ferzah); (v) high cost of freight and container trans-shipment due to the limited number of regular shipping lines; (vi) old fleet of ships and port equipment; (vii) lack of storage and refrigeration services; (viii) weak organization, management and regulatory guidelines in the port and marine sector; (ix) monopoly of telephone services; (x) concentration of communication and postal services in urban areas; (xi) high cost of communications especially internet, cellular and international services; and, (xii) dispersion of population in smaller communities in the rural areas.	(i) Transport and communications value-added is projected to increase by 9.1% per annum over the SFYP and the sector's share in GDP is expected to increase from 10% to 12.2% by 2005; (ii) the plan also aims to increase passenger transport on domestic and international routes by an average of 4% annually and increase air cargo by an average of 10% per annum; (iii) the plan targets building some 4,500 km of asphalt roads and doubling telephone line connections by the end of the plan.	High transportation cost and poor networks is one of the major constraints to economic growth and private sector development in Yemen. Therefore, this sector should receive higher priority in the short and long-terms. Deregulation, liberalization of prices, tariffs and fares, encouraging private sector provision of services, privatization of government monopolies are among the most critical reforms to achieve the SFYP growth targets.	(i) ensure private provision of transport and communications by schemes such as BOT, BOO, etc.; (ii) create regulatory agencies independent from provision of services; (iii) liberalize tariffs and fares in the sector; (iv) privatization of public enterprises into the transport and communications sector; (v) assess the feasibility of establishing a rail (train) networks, particularly to link areas of rich mineral reserves with seaports; and, (vi) complete and maintain existing roads before embarking on construction of new ones.	Further liberalization of the sector, particularly in telecommunications and air and land transport sectors.

3.3. Wholesale and Retail Trade:

MAJOR POTENTIALS	MAJOR CONSTRAINTS	SYFP OBJECTIVES	OBSERVATION & COMMENTS	PROPOSED POLICIES AND REFORM MEASURES	PRIORITY REFORMS
Yemen's large area, different pattern of economic activities among governorates, large population size and high population growth, and	(i) weaknesses in the institutional and regulatory frameworks; (ii) monopolies on certain activities; (iii) smuggling and dumping; (iv) weak trade-related infrastructure and services (e.g.,	Value-added of wholesale and retail trade is planned to increase by 9% per annum over the next five years.	The targets can be achieved if most of the constraints in the sector are addressed.	(i) establish and enforce regulations for consumer protection and safeguards for intellectual and property rights; (ii) end monopolies and unfair competition in the sector, and (iii) improve trade-related services and infrastructure.	Reinforce the legal and judicial frameworks.

Major Potentials	Major Constraints	SYFP Objectives	Observation & Comments	Proposed Policies and Reform Measures	Priority Reforms
favorable outlook for GDP growth are important factors in accelerating domestic trade.	transport, packing, storage, communication, credit); and, (v) lack of quality controls and standards.				

3.4. Government Services and Public Investment:

Major Potentials	Major Constraints	SYFP Objectives	Observation & Comments	Proposed Policies and Reform Measures	Priority Reforms
Given the infancy of the private sector in Yemen and high poverty levels, there is a need and scope for increased and improved government services particularly in the social sectors and some economic sectors.	(i) inefficient and inflated civil services; (ii) inefficient allocation of public resources (high current spending at the expense of maintenance and operations and investment spending); and, (iii) high cost of contracts and procurement and weak financial management.	During SFYP, government services are planned to increase by an annul average of 4.7% and their share in GDP will therefore decline slightly from 10.8% in 2000 to 10.4% by 2005.	(i) real public investment is planned to increase by 12.7% during the plan; (ii) the target of raising the share of investment spending in toral spending from 15% to 18% by 2005 and increasing the relative allocation of government spending on the social sectors are commended; and (iii) the expected decline in the relative allocations on transport is inconsistent with priorities set for the sector.	(i) increase efficiency in the delivery of public services; (ii) redirect resources towards social sectors and infrastructure and away from production and distribution; (iii) complete vigorously and systematically the implementation of the Civil Services Modernization Project; and (iv) accord higher priority to uncompleted projects and to maintenance and operations.	Avoid unsustainable increases in government spending which has been the cause of unsustainable fiscal deficits in the past

4. Productivity and Investment:

Major Potentials	Major Constraints	SYFP Objectives	Observation & Comments	Proposed Policies and Reform Measures	Priority Reforms
(i) there is a wide scope for raising productivity by pursuing structural reforms and even without additional investments; (ii) there are good potentials to attract FDI I oil, gas, mining, manufacturing and into Aden free zones; and (iii) political relations with the GCC countries improved.	(i) TFP was negative for most of the 1990s; (ii) decline in investment ratios to GDP in the late 1990s, and; (iii) the business and investment environment is not conducive to attract private (local and foreign) investors.	SFYP seeks to achieve an increase in total investment from 19.2% of GDP to 29% by 2005. This will depend on achieving a high nominal growth in private investment reaching 23.5%, and 15.1% for public investments (18% for Govt. and 10% for oil sector). Thus, the share of private investment in total investment is expected to rise from 53% in 2000 to 62% by 2005.	(i) negative or low TFP characterizes most of the economic sectors; (ii) there are inconsistencies in the constant price data for investment levels under the plan; (iii) the plan envisages at least an annual increase in total investment by 14.3%; v) sustained improvement in productivity performance depends on success in rapid diversification in economic activity over time, in trade goods and services and away from excessive dependence on resources and commodities such as oil.	(ii) improve the business and investment environment, and (ii) improve the outcomes of the educational and training systems.	Enhance productivity increase by further liberalization and deregulations, privatization of public enterprises.

5. Private Sector Development and Investment:

Major Potentials	Major Constraints	SYFP Objectives	Observation & Comments	Proposed Policies and Reform Measures	Priority Reforms
(i) Yemenis abroad have considerable wealth and investments, good entrepreneurial skills that can be attracted to invest in Yemen; (ii) ongoing reforms in microeconomic policy framework and international trade regime are making an impact on the private sector environment; (iii) Aden port and free zone have promising potentials to attract private sector investments.	(i) inadequate access to high quality, competitive prices infrastructure (roads, telecom and electricity) (ii) shortage of land (iii) regulatory and administrative hurdles; (iv) costly transportation; (v) smuggling and dumping; (vi) marketing and transportation difficulties; (vii) limited access to credit and high cost of financing; (viii) high levels of risk and uncertainty in the general investment climate, (ix) highly complicated and corrupt tax system, and; (x) weak judicial and legal system and law enforcement.	The SFYP aims to raise the share of the private sector in total GDP, and in non-oil GDP to 53.7% and 72.3% respectively by 2005 or a real growth in private sector value-added of 10% average annual rate of 10% over the coming five years.	(i) in real terms, private investment is projected to increase by an annual average of 21%. This seems unrealistic in the current business and investment environment; (ii) value-added of the private sector continued to decline as a share of GDP and non-oil GDP in the late 1990s there are no indications in the SFYP about sources to finance the envisaged additional investment; and; (iii) private investment which peaked at 20% in 1997 continued to decline in the subsequent three years reaching only 10% by 2000.	(i) reduce policy uncertainty (macro-fiscal, structural and firm specific uncertainties); (ii) improve the quality of public services (roads, electricity, *et*) and (iii) improve financial intermediation (see Chapter 3 for details).	Improve governance and market institutions by strengthening accountability of the public sector, better formal legal and contract enforcement systems, and reduction of regulatory and administrative hurdles.

6. External Trade and Export Competitiveness:

Major Potentials	Major Constraints	SYFP Objectives	Observation & Comments	Proposed Policies and Reform Measures	Priority Reforms
(i) Yemen is one of the most	(i) dominance of oil exports and	The SFYP projects an	Breakdown of exports is not available	(i) maintain the policy of flexible exchange rate regime;	Continue and

Major Potentials	Major Constraints	SYFP Objectives	Observation & Comments	Proposed Policies and Reform Measures	Priority Reforms
open and trade-liberalized economies in MENA; (ii) major improvements in competitiveness and performance of non-oil exports in the 1990s; (iii) improved political relations with the GCC countries; and (iv) manufacturing export capacity is not fully utilized.	vulnerability to fluctuations in oil prices; (ii) non-oil exports depend on a limited number of commodities; (iii) high degree of market concentration and high degree of vulnerability of exports to the outlook in emerging markets; (iv) poor quality and sanitary standards; (v) low value of exports of primary commodities.	annual decline in merchandise exports by 2.5% in the coming five years.	but it seems that the assumption of annual decline in merchandise exports is based on the assumption of annual decline in oil exports.	(i) enhance trade-related infrastructure and services (transport, access to credit, promotion, *etc.*); (iii) enhance quality of products and enforce sanitary and other quality standards; and (iv) increase processing of raw agricultural commodities to increase value added (fish, coffee, *etc.*).	further trade liberalization policies.

ANNEXES

Annex Table 1: Share of Services Sector in Yemen's GDP and Its Contribution to GDP Growth, 1991-2000 (%)

	Total Services Value-Added				Administration (Govt. Services)				Trade (Wholesale and Retail)				Transport & Storage				Real Estate & Business Sector				Banking (Financial Institutions)			
	Growth rate	Share in GDP	Contribution to GDP growth	Share in GDP Growth	Growth rate	Share in GDP	Contribution to GDP growth	Share in GDP Growth	Growth rate	Share in GDP	Contribution to GDP growth	Share in GDP Growth	Growth rate	Share in GDP	Contribution to GDP growth	Share in GDP Growth	Growth rate	Share in GDP	Contribution to GDP growth	Share in GDP Growth	Growth rate	Share in GDP	Contribution to GDP growth	Share in GDP Growth
1991	7.8	54.2	3.8	193.5	18.8	16.7	2.9	147.6	4.8	8.2	0.3	16.4	-6.0	14.8	-0.9	-44.9	5.5	5.9	0.3	14.9	2.3	4.5	0.1	3.4
1992	9.9	54.3	5.4	64.6	20.8	16.9	3.5	41.7	1.7	8.3	0.1	1.6	17.4	15.5	2.6	31.1	3.3	6.1	0.2	2.4	-12.9	3.7	-0.6	-6.9
1993	3.7	56.8	2.0	49.6	13.2	17.2	2.2	54.9	6.9	9.1	0.6	14.0	-13.9	16.7	-2.2	-53.0	5.4	6.3	0.3	8.1	0.3	3.8	0.0	0.3
1994	-0.2	53.4	-0.1	-4.0	13.6	15.9	2.3	108.0	-13.2	9.8	-1.2	-55.5	-19.2	14.6	-3.2	-148.5	4.3	6.1	0.3	12.4	8.6	4.5	0.3	15.0
1995	7.4	48.4	3.9	36.3	12.7	12.9	2.0	18.5	15.5	9.7	1.5	14.0	-2.8	12.6	-0.4	-3.8	5.1	5.9	0.3	2.9	-9.0	3.7	-0.4	-3.8
1996	5.0	41.9	2.4	41.4	8.0	10.0	1.0	17.6	8.2	8.0	0.8	13.5	-14.0	11.3	-1.8	-30.1	5.7	5.9	0.3	5.7	-24.1	2.3	-0.9	-15.1
1997	8.1	40.9	3.4	41.9	7.7	9.2	0.8	9.6	6.6	8.2	0.5	6.6	18.3	11.9	2.1	25.5	6.2	5.3	0.4	4.6	-1.0	2.0	0.0	-0.3
1998	2.4	47.9	1.0	19.8	0.9	11.0	0.1	1.7	8.2	9.2	0.7	13.7	6.3	14.3	0.7	15.2	6.4	6.4	0.3	7.0	61.8	3.6	1.2	24.8
1999	4.8	41.1	2.3	61.6	5.9	10.5	0.6	17.6	-2.2	7.4	-0.2	-5.5	2.0	11.6	0.3	7.8	6.3	5.6	0.4	10.9	24.1	3.4	0.9	23.6
2000	4.7	38.4	1.9	37.4	5.9	10.8	0.6	12.1	9.2	7.2	0.7	13.3	1.0	10.3	0.1	0.0	6.4	4.9	0.4	6.9	-8.6	2.9	-0.3	-5.8

Source: World Bank, Live Database, LDB, 2001.

Annex Table 2: Share of Industrial Sector in Yemen's GDP and Its Contribution to GDP Growth, 1991-2000 (%)

	Total Industrial Value-Added				Mining & Quarrying				Gas, Electricity and Water				Construction				Manufacturing			
	Growth rate	Share in GDP	Contribution to GDP growth	Share in GDP Growth	Growth rate	Share in GDP	Contribution to GDP growth	Share in GDP Growth	Growth rate	Share in GDP	Contribution to GDP growth	Share in GDP Growth	Growth rate	Share in GDP	Contribution to GDP growth	Share in GDP Growth	Growth rate	Share in GDP	Contribution to GDP growth	Share in GDP Growth
1991	-0.2	24.5	0.0	-2.2	-5.6	10.0	-0.8	-38.6	13.9	1.2	0.2	8.2	8.1	3.2	0.2	11.1	3.6	10.1	0.3	17.0
1992	-3.9	22.7	-0.9	-11.4	-15.4	7.1	-1.5	-18.6	1.9	1.0	0.0	0.3	17.0	3.6	0.5	6.4	4.4	11.0	0.4	5.4
1993	4.5	21.8	1.0	25.0	4.2	5.6	0.3	7.4	1.8	0.9	0.0	0.4	1.7	3.4	0.1	1.5	6.0	12.0	0.7	16.2
1994	13.1	24.0	2.9	132.6	42.7	6.1	2.4	110.6	-10.3	0.7	-0.1	-4.2	-17.2	3.7	-0.6	-26.8	-5.3	13.6	-0.6	-29.5
1995	21.2	32.2	5.1	47.0	19.9	13.8	1.2	11.2	13.6	0.6	0.1	0.8	23.1	3.5	0.9	7.8	23.7	14.3	3.2	29.8
1996	10.5	41.9	3.4	57.6	13.5	26.3	1.9	31.8	12.3	0.7	0.1	1.3	28.2	3.9	1.0	16.8	0.6	10.9	0.1	1.5
1997	7.6	43.6	3.2	39.4	7.5	27.8	2.0	24.3	2.0	0.8	0.0	0.2	28.4	4.6	1.1	13.9	1.1	10.4	0.1	1.4
1998	2.7	32.8	1.2	24.1	2.5	16.4	0.7	14.1	2.4	0.9	0.0	0.4	1.4	5.2	0.1	1.4	3.8	10.2	0.4	8.0
1999	4.8	42.8	1.6	42.3	7.8	29.2	1.3	34.7	7.2	0.7	0.1	1.8	0.7	4.7	0.0	1.0	0.7	8.2	0.1	1.9
2000	7.0	46.2	3.0	58.4	7.2	33.8	2.1	41.0	6.5	0.7	0.0	0.9	8.2	4.2	0.4	7.5	6.1	7.5	0.5	9.8

Source: World Bank, Live Database, LDB, 2001.

ANNEX TABLE 3: SHARE OF AGRICULTURAL SECTOR IN YEMEN'S GDP AND ITS CONTRIBUTION TO GDP GROWTH, 1991-2000 (%)

Year	Total Agricultural Value-Added			Agriculture and Forestry				O/w Qat				Fishing			
	Growth rate	Contribution to GDP growth	Share in GDP Growth	Growth rate	Share in GDP	Contribution to GDP growth	Share in GDP Growth	Growth rate	Share in GDP	Contribution to GDP growth	Share in GDP Growth	Growth rate	Share in GDP	Contribution to GDP growth	Share in GDP Growth
1991	-7.4	-1.8	-91.2	-9.0	20.4	-2.1	-108.1	0.4	8.1	0.0	1.8	52.8	0.9	0.3	16.9
1992	19.1	4.1	48.9	19.1	22.1	3.9	46.8	0.7	7.4	0.1	0.7	19.0	1.0	0.2	2.1
1993	4.4	1.0	25.2	4.7	20.5	1.0	25.5	11.9	7.4	0.9	21.7	-1.4	0.9	0.0	-0.3
1994	-3.4	-0.7	-33.7	-7.8	20.7	-1.6	-73.8	-12.4	7.1	-0.9	-42.3	100.2	1.9	0.9	40.1
1995	6.9	1.6	14.4	6.3	17.7	1.3	12.1	-4.9	5.4	-0.3	-3.2	13.3	1.7	0.3	2.3
1996	1.9	0.4	6.1	1.8	14.7	0.3	5.4	7.0	4.7	0.4	6.4	2.6	1.5	0.0	0.8
1997	8.8	1.4	17.6	8.0	14.0	1.2	14.6	6.0	4.4	0.3	3.5	16.4	1.5	0.2	3.0
1998	13.7	2.1	43.5	14.6	17.7	2.1	41.9	7.4	5.2	0.3	6.7	5.2	1.7	0.1	1.6
1999	0.2	0.0	0.9	1.7	14.9	0.3	7.9	1.8	4.4	0.1	2.6	-15.1	1.2	-0.3	-7.0
2000	3.7	0.6	11.6	3.7	14.2	0.6	10.9	4.1	4.2	0.2	3.5	3.0	1.1	0.0	0.7

Source: World Bank, Live Database, LDB, 2001.

ANNEX TABLE 4: INTERNATIONAL AND DOMESTIC BED-NIGHTS IN 3, 4 AND 5 STAR HOTELS, 1995-2000

Year	Europe	Middle East	Total
1995	306,755	627,525	934,280
1996	365,830	634,320	1,000,150
1997	482,706	829,894	1,312,600
1998	525,762	904,458	1,430,220
1999	379,405	943,105	1,322,510
2000	473,434	1,169,876	1,643,310

Source: Data from the General Tourism Authority, 2001.

ANNEX TABLE 5: TOURIST ARRIVALS BY AVERAGE LENGTH OF STAY AND DAILY EXPENDITURES, 1995-2000

Year	Total arrivals	Average length of stay	Total bed nights	Average daily expenditure	Total Expenditures	
					RY million	US$ million
1995	61,351	6.0	306,755	US$ 160	6,250	50
1996	74,476	5.0	365,830	US$ 150	6,870	55
1997	80,451	6.0	482,706	US$ 145	8,970	69
1998	87,627	6.0	525,762	US$ 160	11,729	84
1999	58,370	6.5	379,405	US$ 160	9,774	61
2000	73,836	6.5	473,434	US$ 160	12,540	76

Source: Data from the General Tourism Authority, 2001.

ANNEX TABLE 6: HOTEL ROOMS BY CLASS, 1995–2000

Year	5*	4*	3*	2*	1*	Unclassified	Total
1995	656	416	1691	1500	1863	393	6519
1996	646	418	1808	1495	2147	463	6977
1997	646	458	1928	1675	2467	523	7696
1998	646	828	2105	1893	2719	608	8799
1999	842	1275	2037	1903	2754	934	9765
2000	1056	1533	1998	1972	2307	1574	10440

Source: Data from the General Tourism Authority, 2001.

ANNEX TABLE 7: TOURISM ESTABLISHMENTS BY TYPE AND GOVERNORATE

Governorate	1	2	3	4	Total
Capital City	309	180	15	135	639
Aden	88	82	19	47	236
Taiz	130	337	2	9	478
Hadramout	76	43	11	23	153
Hodeidah	65	63	4	8	140
Lahj	25	46	1	1	73
Ibb	16	70	1	3	90
Abyan	12	4	-	4	20
Hajjah	31	33	1	-	65
Sadah	37	38	4	-	79
Marib	3	10	1	1	15
Shabwah	9	21	-	3	33
Al-Mahweet	1	7	2	3	13
Sana'a	13	3	2	12	30
Dhamar	12	14	1	3	30
Amran	9	3	-	-	12
Al-Mahra	8	3	-	-	11
Al-Baidha	12	3	-	-	15
Al-Dhala	27	7	2	1	37
Total	863	987	66	253	2169

Source: Data obtained from the General Tourism Authority, Sana'a, 2001.

1 = hotels and other accommodation facilities   3 = clubs and amusement parks
2 = restaurants and similar establishments   4 = tour operators and travel agencies

ANNEX TABLE 8: GROWTH OF MANUFACTURING SUB-SECTORS, 1990-2000 (%)

	1991	1992	1993	1994	1995	1996	1997	1998	1999	2000
Food Processing	1.3	1.3	1.9	-6.6	37.6	5.4	-2.2	8.3	-1.7	6.3
Textiles, Clothing & Leather	3.1	9.4	11.9	-1.5	14.3	-34.9	-8.8	35.4	0.2	3.3
Wooden and Furniture	8.2	11.4	7.3	-1.4	17.7	-11.5	2.4	2.6	0.6	2.8
Paper & Printing	0.2	9.6	21.6	-4.4	9.0	-17.6	6.4	6.5	5.2	2.0
Chemicals and Plastic	0.1	0.2	0.8	-8.7	9.1	-5.1	-6.7	17.1	1.2	3.4
Non-metallic (Construction)	6.1	7.6	13.4	-3.7	38.1	13.5	8.4	6.0	2.8	11.4
Metal Products, Machinery and Equipment	12.0	13.8	10.1	0.3	17.5	7.7	2.9	-19.0	0.8	3.5
Oil Refining	3.2	0.3	0.3	-9.5	6.4	-3.8	0.4	-6.4	1.5	-0.4
Total Manufacturing (including Oil Refining)	3.6	4.4	6.0	-5.3	23.7	0.6	1.1	3.8	0.7	5.8
Manufacturing (excluding oil refining)	3.7	5.5	7.4	-4.4	27.6	1.4	1.2	5.5	0.6	6.8
GDP	2.0	8.3	4.1	2.2	10.9	5.9	8.1	4.9	3.7	5.1

Source: Data from the National Accounts, Central Statistical Organization (CSO), 2000.

ANNEX TABLE 9: PROJECTED OIL PRODUCTION LEVELS, 2001-2010 FROM EXISTING FIELDS

Year	Sector 18 Marib-Al-Jouf		Sector 24 - Al-Masila		Sector 10 - Eastern Shabwah		Sector 5 – Jannah		Sector 36 - Hawarim		Sector 53 - Eastern Samar		Sector 4 - Ayad		Total Average Production	Total Annual Production
	Daily Production	Annual Production	Daily Production	Annual Production	Daily Production	Annual Production	Daily Production	Annual Production	Daily Production	Annual Production	Daily Production	Annual Production	Daily Production	Annual Production		
2001	112	40.9	230.6	84.2	285	10.4	58	21.2	8.2	3	15	0.68	0.54	0.2	440	160.5
2002	102	37.2	230	84	31	11	57	20.8	9	3.3	19	6.9	0.5	0.2	448	163.3
2003	86	31.4	229	83.6	315	11.5	51.6	18.8	7	2.6	11.3	4.1	0.5	0.2	417	152.2
2004	69	25.2	229	83.6	208	7.6	46.7	17	5.5	2	6.7	2.4	0.5	0.2	378	138
2005	55	20.1	228	83.2	127	4.6	37.5	13.7	4.3	1.6	4.8	1.8	0.5	0.2	343	125.1
2006	44	16.1	198	72.3	10.12	3.7	30.1	11.0	3.3	1.2	3.6	1.3	0.5	0.2	286	105.7
2007	35	12.8	164	59.9	8.55	3.1	24.1	8.8	2.7	1.0	2.9	1.1	0.5	0.2	238	86.8
2008	28	10.2	139	50.7	6.66	2.4	19.4	7.1	2.2	0.8	2.4	0.9	0.5	0.2	198	72.3
2009	23	8.4	121	44.2	5.20	1.9	15.5	5.7	1.8	0.7	2.0	0.9	0.5	0.2	169	61.7
2010	18	6.6	105	38.3	4.23	1.5	12.5	4.6	1.5	0.5	1.7	0.6	0.5	0.2	143	52.4
Total		208.9		684.0		57.7		128.7		16.7		20.7		2.0		111.8

Annual Production figures are in millions of barrels per day and average daily production are in thousands of barrels per day.

Source: Data provided by the Ministry of Oil and Minerals (December 2001)

ANNEX TABLE 10: TARGETS FOR GDP AND DEMAND COMPONENTS OF THE SECOND FIVE-YEAR PLAN
(Billions of Yemeni Rials, unless otherwise stated)

	1995	2000	2001	2002	2003	2004	2005	Average Annual Growth Rate, 2000-2005 (%)
At Current Prices								
GDP at Market Prices	511	1,380	1,512	1,660	1,836	2,050	2,285	10.6
Imports of Goods and Services	216	572	618	664	711	757	802	7.0
Total Final Consumption	502	991	1,106	1,230	1,363	1,503	1,655	10.8
Public Consumption	74	194	219	247	276	308	342	12.0
Total Private Consumption	428	797	887	983	1,086	1,195	1,313	10.5
Total Investment	113	264	339	407	480	570	654	19.9
Formation of Fixed Capital	106	252	323	388	458	543	623	19.9
Changes in Stock Difference	6	13	16	19	23	27	31	20.0
Exports of Goods and Services	112	696	685	688	703	734	778	2.23
At Constant 2000 Prices using projected GDP Deflator								
GDP at Market Prices	1,054	1,380	1,445	1,529	1,631	1,749	1,884	6.4
Goods and Services Imports	445	572	591	612	631	646	661	2.9
Total Final Consumption	1,124	991	1,058	1,133	1,210	1,283	1,365	6.6
Public Consumption	166	194	210	227	246	263	282	7.8
Total Private Consumption	959	797	848	906	965	1,020	1,083	6.3
Total Investment	141	264	324	374	427	486	539	15.3
Formation of Fixed Capital	133	252	309	357	406	463	513	15.3
Changes in Stock Difference	8	13	15	18	20	23	26	15.5
Goods and Services Exports	235	696	654	634	625	626	641	-1.4
GDP Deflator (%)			4.6	3.8	3.7	4.1	3.5	3.9
At Constant 2000 Prices using CPI Inflation Rate								
GDP at Market Prices	1,054	1,380	1,430	1,496	1,582	1,683	1,799	5.5
Goods and Services Imports	445	572	584	598	612	621	632	2.0
Total Final Consumption	1,124	991	1,047	1,108	1,174	1,234	1,304	5.6
Public Consumption	166	194	208	222	238	253	269	6.8
Total Private Consumption	959	797	839	886	936	981	1,034	5.3
Total Investment	141	264	321	366	414	468	515	14.3
Formation of Fixed Capital	133	252	306	349	394	446	490	14.3
Changes in Stock Difference	8	13	15	17	20	22	25	14.4
Goods and Services Exports	235	696	648	620	606	602	613	-2.3
CPI (%)			5.7	5.0	4.6	4.9	4.30	4.9

Sources: SFYP (2001) and staff estimates.

ANNEX TABLE 11: LEGAL ORGANIZATION OF FIRMS

	No.	Valid (%)
Single Proprietorship	777	83.46
Partnership	100	10.74
Corporation	41	4.40
Cooperative	3	0.32
Other	10	1.07
No response/can't answer	16	
Total	947	100.00

Source: Data from the Private Sector Survey undertook by the World Bank, November 2001.

ANNEX TABLE 12: SECTOR OF ACTIVITY, PRIVATE SECTOR FIRMS, 2001

Sector	No.	Valid (%)
Manufacturing	209	22.59
Services	559	60.43
Other	84	9.08
Conglomerate (>1 answer)	73	7.89
No response	22	
Total	947	100.00

Sector 2 digit	No.	Valid %
Heavy Industry	4	0.43
Consumer Goods	31	3.35
Garments	41	4.43
Food and Beverages	25	2.70
Leather & Shoes	3	0.32
Other Manufacturing	105	11.35
Tourism, hotels, restaurants	27	2.92
Trade: retail/wholesale	271	29.30
Transport and storage	9	0.97
Finance and banking	13	1.41
Personal services	33	3.57
Other Services	206	22.27
Agriculture	11	1.19
Fishing	1	0.11
Extraction (mining, oil)	3	0.32
Construction	20	2.16
Electricity, gas, water	11	1.19
Other	38	4.11
Conglomerate (>1 answer)	73	7.89
No response	22	
Total	947	100.00

Source: Data from the Private Sector Survey undertook by the World Bank, November 2001.

ANNEX TABLE 13: PRIVATE SECTOR'S ASSESSMENT OF EFFICIENCY OF GOVERNMENT SERVICES

Government Services		Sana'a	Aden	Taiz	Hodeidah	Hadramout
Very efficient/Efficient	No.	34	37	31	8	23
	%	14.0	15.9	16.7	8.1	19.0
Somewhat efficient	No.	117	62	83	47	65
	%	48.3	26.7	44.6	47.5	53.7
Somewhat inefficient	No.	54	52	18	25	16
	%	22.3	22.4	9.7	25.3	13.2
Inefficient/Very Inefficient	No.	37	81	54	19	17
	%	15.3	34.9	29.0	19.2	14.0

Source: Data from the Private Sector Survey undertook by the World Bank, November 2001.

ANNEX TABLE 14: OWNERSHIP OF LAND, PRIVATE SECTOR SURVEY

	Yes	No	No response /can't say	Total
Sana'a	99	157	9	265
Hodeidah	42	64		106
Aden	84	163	2	249
Taiz	46	146	8	200
Hadramout	16	110	1	127
Total	287	640	20	947

Source: Data from the Private Sector Survey undertook by the World Bank, November 2001.

ANNEX TABLE 15: ENTRY COSTS
Time, Official and Unofficial Costs of Establishing Business in Yemen

Time (months)	Electricity Connection	Telephone Connection	Water Connection	Business License	Municipal Permits	Total Start Up
N	43	37	26	60	42	49
Minimum	0	0	0	0	0	0
Maximum	12	12	12	10	10	24
Median	1	1	1	1	1	3
Mean	2.16	2.19	2.19	1.57	1.9	4.78
Std. Dev.	3.09	2.78	3.37	1.54	2.47	4.88

Official Costs (Rials)	Electricity Connection	Telephone Connection	Water Connection	Business License	Municipal Permits	Total Start Up
N	37	38	20	60	42	28
Minimum	0	0	0	0	0	5000
Maximum	500,000	255,000	100,000	200,000	50,000	3,000,000
Median	20,000	26,000	10,000	5,000	5,000	450,000
Mean	55,473	44,453	16,583	11,635	8,429	639,500
Std. Dev.	99,868	48,379	24,303	26,273	9,244	667,945

Unofficial Costs (Rials)	Electricity Connection	Telephone Connection	Water Connection	Business License	Municipal Permits	Total Start Up
N	27	19	10	35	25	11
Minimum	0	0	0	0	0	0
Maximum	70,000	30,000	20,000	50,000	20,000	400,000
Median	5,000	3,000	1,500	2,000	3,000	2,000
Mean	12,333	5,632	5,300	6,623	4,314	57,818
Std. Dev.	18,833	7,253	6,865	12,099	5,054	121,305

Source: Data from the Private Sector Survey undertook by the World Bank, November 2001.

ANNEX TABLE 16: DELAYS IN BUREAUCRATIC INTERACTIONS
(Number of day's delays to get/deal with)

Days	Connect to Public Services		Get Licenses and Permits		Deal with Tax Authorities		Get Government Contracts		Clear Customs		Buy Land/Constr. Permit	
	N	Valid %	N	Valid %	N	Valid %	N	Valid %	N	Valid %	N	Valid %
0	11	3.54	8	1.97	10	2.5	50	45.87	45	23.56	26	23.21
1-5 days	87	27.97	158	38.92	170	42.5	7	6.42	77	40.31	15	13.39
6-10 days	49	15.76	130	32.02	77	19.25	7	6.42	43	22.51	12	10.71
11-20 days	28	9	50	12.32	38	9.5	12	11.01	14	7.33	7	6.25
21-50 days	69	22.19	36	8.87	45	11.25	7	6.42	7	3.66	17	15.18
51-100 days	39	12.54	15	3.69	35	8.75	18	16.51	3	1.57	20	17.86
>100 days	28	9	9	2.22	25	6.25	8	7.34	2	1.05	15	13.39
Total	311	100	406	100.01	400	100	109	99.99	191	99.99	112	99.99
Mean	30.28		12.62		21.25		26.23		6.3		30.5	
Median	15		7		7		2		3		10	

Source: Data from the Private Sector Survey undertook by the World Bank, November 2001.

ANNEX TABLE 17: EMPLOYMENT IN THE OIL SECTOR

	Units	Yemeni Employees	Non-Yemeni Employees
Oil Companies in Production Stages	7	2,426	514
Oil Companies in Exploration Stages	20	346	55
Subcontractors & Companies in Oil Services	42	2,814	777
Ministry of Oil and Minerals & Associated Units	10	12,213	0
Total	79	17,799	1,346

Source: Data provided by the Ministry of Oil and Minerals, 22 April 2002.

ANNEX A: NATIONAL ACCOUNTS DATA

NATIONAL ACCOUNTS STATISTICS IN YEMEN

The National Accounts Division of the Central Statistics Organization (CSO) compiles national accounts statistics in Yemen. The estimates are based on the concepts and classifications of the *System of National Accounts* 1968. [80] The CSO produces and disseminates the following data on an annual basis covering the calendar year: (i) GDP at current market prices by 11 major industrial activities and 17 sub-activities; (iii) GDP at current prices by the following expenditure categories (private and public final consumption expenditures, gross capital formation (no distinction between private and government components), changes in inventory for the total economy, exports and imports; (iii) GDP at constant prices (base year 1990) by 11 major industrial activities and 17 sub-activities without expenditure categories. In addition, data are also produced and disseminated on gross national income, gross disposable income and domestic and national saving. GDP estimates are also complied annually for the whole economy using the production approach at current and constant prices following the same industrial classification.

The definition and concepts of the Yemen national accounts follow primarily the 1968 SNA, but a number of features of the *1993 SNA* are being implemented whenever possible. Value-added by industrial activity is calculated on gross production less intermediate consummation. GDP by expenditure category is calculated as the sum of the final use of goods and services through final consumption, gross capital formation and exports less imports.

Industrial activity is classified and estimates published according to the International Standard Industrial Classification (ISIC of all Economic Activities, Revision 3) except for services and government activities. The 15 ISIC categories are used with sub-activities as follows: agriculture, hunting and forestry (excluding Qat); fishing; other agriculture, hunting and forestry (including Qat); mining and quarrying; crude oil and gas; other mining and quarrying; manufacturing, oil refining; other manufacturing; electricity, gas and water supply; buildings and construction; wholesale and retile trade; hotels and restaurants; transport, storage and communication; financial intermediation; real estate and business services; community, social and personal services; producers of government services, and private non-profit institutions serving households.

SOURCES OF DATA ON NATIONAL ACCOUNTS USED IN THIS REPORT

This Report utilizes mainly the new set of revised national accounts prepared by the Central Statistical Organization (CSO). The new set of national accounts, which was released in September 2000 (again updated in March 2001 and March 2002), updated national accounts in the old set, which was released in October 1999. The major differences have been: (i) an increase in the estimates of construction activity by an annual average of 8%; (ii) addition of maintenance to the national accounts and higher estimates for restaurant and hotels (as a result wholesale and retail trade estimates increased); (iii) slight revision in the

---

[80] This section draws on the IMF, Statistical Department, National Accounts Draft List of Prompt Points Reports, 23 October 1999.

estimates for transport, communication and storage in 1997 and 1998; (iv) major revision in the estimation of financial institutions and real estate; (v) reduction in the estimates of community and social services; (vi) major changes in the estimation of government services particularly in the late 1990s; (vii) and higher estimates for private non-profit services.

As a result of these revisions, real GDP estimates were increased by about 19% on average (and higher in the late 1990s). Most of the revisions resulted in higher estimates of non-oil GDP. The Table below provides annual percentage changes in the estimates of national accounts between the new set and the old set.

ANNEX TABLE 18: PERCENTAGE CHANGES BETWEEN NEW AND OLD SETS OF NATIONAL ACCOUNTS

Item	1990	1991	1992	1993	1994	1995	1996	1997	1998
Construction	4%	6%	7%	6%	8%	7%	13%	10%	11%
Wholesale and Retail Trade	14%	14%	14%	14%	17%	15%	15%	14%	15%
Restaurants and Hotels	44%	51%	50%	51%	53%	53%	53%	46%	47%
Maintenance	N/A	N/A	N/A	N/A	N/A	N/A	N/A	N/A	N/A
Transport, Storage & Communications	0%	0%	0%	0%	0%	0%	0%	2%	12%
Financial Institutions & Real Estate	51%	50%	53%	54%	51%	53%	62%	62%	52%
Real Estate & Business Services	111%	104%	101%	100%	97%	93%	95%	93%	92%
Community Social & Personal services	-32%	-29%	-31%	-31%	-32%	-34%	-30%	-32%	-30%
Government Services	0%	26%	52%	84%	156%	233%	316%	325%	307%
Private Non -Profit services	105%	160%	115%	300%	453%	188%	397%	416%	463%
GDP at Market Prices	**4%**	**8%**	**11%**	**16%**	**22%**	**26%**	**29%**	**29%**	**29%**
Non -Oil GDP	4%	9%	13%	18%	27%	32%	37%	37%	37%

Source: Staff estimates based on national accounts data from the Central Statistical Organization (CSO).

On the demand side, the revisions in the national accounts provides for higher estimates in the final consumption and expenditures, in particular in private consumption. Gross domestic investments were also revised upwards in the late 1990s.

RELIABILITY OF THE DATA

Although significant progress has been made in revising national accounts in Yemen, there is still a long way to go until the country adopts the 1993 SNA. The current system suffers from a number of deficiencies in terms of coverage, estimation, reconciliation, compilation and classification. Currently, the national accounts cover the whole territory of Yemen and cover, in principle, the economic activities of all Yemen residents in conformity of the 1968 SNA. However, no adjustment is made to impute the value of informal activities.

With regard to transaction coverage, at present estimates are limited to value added by economic activity in current and constant prices and expenditure in current prices for the total economy. Estimates are produced for GNP, gross disposable income, gross domestic saving and gross national saving. Fixed capital formation includes construction, machinery and equipment. There are no separate accounts showing instructional or consolidated transactions on income and outlay and capital finance. Most transactions are recorded on the accrual basis in conformity with the 1968 SNA but government and financial sector transactions are largely on a cash basis. Output is valued at producers' prices and domestic uses are valued at purchasers' prices. Imports are valued c.i.f and exports are valued f.o.b.

GDP by production approach is based on a variety of sources, censuses surveys and administrative records that are available annually or at some periodic intervals. Ad hoc data sources through surveys or special studies are also used as benchmark estimate or as basis for deriving estimation parameters for indirect estimation.

The CSO has an ambitious program to address the current deficiencies in the system of national accounts A project for improving national accounts of Yemen (during 1999-2003) was developed in collaboration with the IMF Statistics Departments. The Dutch government is also providing assistance in data sources and training though the project of "Strengthening the Institutional Structure and Capacity of the CSO". In the short-term, the CSO hopes to rebase the CPI using the 1998 HBS weights and revise the coverage of the index, revise the national accounts and rebase them to 1998 or a more recent year, improve the coverage of GDP, initiate work on intuitional sector accounts and use international classification, focusing on the household, government and financial corporation, enhance computerization and develop constant estimates for GDP by expenditures. In the medium term, the CSO plans to develop a producer price index and foreign trade indices, improve the methodology to estimate gross capital formation and restructure production sector according to ISIC Revision 3 as recommended in the 1993 SNA, conduct new surveys to enhance use of direct methods for GDP estimation, and start the implementation of the 1993 SNA.

DIVERGENCE IN THE ESTIMATES OF PRIVATE CONSUMPTION

As an example for the reliability of the national accounts, there has been a big difference in the estimates for private consumption expenditures in the national accounts and the 1998 HBS.

In Yemen's national accounts, private consumption expenditure consists of the value of final consumption expenditures on goods ad services by households and private non-profit institutions serving households. Private consumption is first estimated as the residual taking GDP by production as control total, separate direct estimates are made using data from the 1992 household budget survey. Furthermore, as private consumption is determined as a residual in the current and constant price accounts; the estimates from the production and expenditures approaches are not independently determined and reconciled by definition. Therefore, any underestimation in the national accounts will undoubtedly be reflected in low private consumption expenditures levels.

Taking 1998 for comparison, the HBS reveals that per capita expenditures in Yemen were about YR 4,436 (YR 5,396 for urban population and YR 4,148 for rural population). Estimates of the national accounts for the same year show per capita private consumption expenditure about YR 3,201. There could be different reasons for the variation but the underestimation of national accounts for GDP (e.g., due to exclusion of informal activities) would be one of the most important factors (see the forthcoming World Bank Poverty Update for Yemen).

ANNEX B: POPULATION GROWTH ESTIMATES IN YEMEN

DIFFERENCES IN ESTIMATES OF POPULATION GROWTH RATE IN YEMEN IN THE 1990

Population estimates for Yemen made by the government and other international agencies vary substantially. The government uses a high population growth rate of **3.7%** in the 1990s based on UN calculations (e.g., UN Population Division's 1996 version) while the World Bank uses a much lower population growth rate of **2.7%**. The difference is largely due to the use of lower total fertility rate (TFR) by the Bank and not to differences in projection models.

In general, the World Bank estimates of population growth rates in member countries rely on UN estimates when reliable country estimates are not available. When there are reliable country estimates, the Bank uses the country data. In countries where new censuses or demographic surveys are available that have not been used in the UN calculations, the Bank updates the UN baseline estimates. Examples in the MENA region where the Bank has different figures from the UN because of utilization of later census data are Egypt, Iran, and Yemen.

According to the World Bank population estimates and projections, based on the 1994 census and the 1997 Demographic Household Survey (DHS), the rate of population growth in the late 1990s was far below the estimates of the UN and the GoY. The 1997 DHS gives a TFR of 6.7 births per woman and the Bank projections assume that the TFR will continue to fall (to 5.55 –the SFYP uses a TFR of 5.9 for 2001). The result is a natural population growth rate of 2.78%, and a total population growth rate (net of assumed emigration of 0.08%) of 2.7% p. a. However, GoY uses the constant TFR of 7.6 and the resulting estimate of population growth rate is 3.7%.

METHODOLOGIES FOR ESTIMATION TFR AND POPULATION GROWTH

Generally, data of the 1994 census are thought to be accurate after adjustment for age heaping. However, the census does do not provide estimates about the current growth rate; it can provide an average intercensal (e.g., 1986-1994) growth rate, but no growth rates in any of the intercensal years (which was highly irregular because of migration). Therefore, projection models use estimates of fertility and mortality and apply them to the census age structure to obtain population growth rates for intercensal years, as well as for years after the most recent census.

There are no differences in the models for projecting population growth rates. These models use population by age and sex, age-specific fertility and mortality schedules, and net migration. The age-specific fertility rates are usually derived from surveys and then applied to the estimated number of women of reproductive age to give the number of births at each age. Similarly, mortality rates at each age are multiplied with the population at each age (including males this time) to calculate the number of deaths. The estimated number of births is divided by the mid-year population to give the crude birth rate; the same calculation for deaths gives the crude death rate. The difference between the two is the rate of natural increase, which, in the absence of migration, equals the population growth rate. If estimates for these inputs are the same, all models will produce the same population growth rate.

Therefore, the differences in estimating TFR, or to a lesser extent, differences in the size of baseline age groups, are responsible for variations in the population growth estimates.

TFR Estimates

Fertility trends in all countries are assumed to continue to fall (because of delays in the age at marriage, education, family planning, etc.) until they reach a replacement level in the future (of about 2). The year of reaching the replacement level is not an arbitrary decision, but the result of applying the rate of change in the fertility rate to future fertility (i.e., an outcome of the extrapolated trend). For Yemen, the choice of the year has no effect on the 1997 growth rate.

The GoY (based on the UN calculations) uses a constant TFR of 7.6 for 1990-2000 that was obtained from the 1991-92 DHS. The GoY estimates do not include the findings from the 1997 DHS. Only after 2005 does the UN show a decline, and then only to 7.35 for the period 2005-10, while the 1997 DHS already shows a TFR of 6.7 for 1992-97. The UN did not have the 1994 census data available for its 1996 version and uses instead projections from the 1986 census and other old sources, which were quite different from the 1994 count. The Bank, on the other hand, uses a lower TFR of 6.7 for the 1990s based on the findings of the 1997 DHS. In the long run, the impact of using very high fertility rates in demographic projections leads to implausible results: recent UN projections for 2050 show the total population for Yemen at 102.3 million.

Census Age Structure

The 1994 census age structure reflects some inaccuracy in age reporting and is greatly different from the one used by the UN and previously by the Bank. The tendency to report age as ending on zero or 5 is stronger in Yemen than in many other countries. Therefore, there is a need to adjust this age structure, reallocating the excesses from ages ending in 0 and 5 to adjoining years in which there are deficits. There are various ways to do this (e.g., using annual growth rates for single year cohorts, and/or by using moving averages); the exact way is not crucial for the purpose of estimating growth rates. Once the single year age structure has been adjusted, 5-year age groups are obtained by aggregation.

ANNEX TABLE 19: POPULATION STRUCTURE IN YEMEN FOR AGE 3-12 YEARS

Age	Total	Males	Females
3	532,605	268,010	264,595
4	565,701	287,662	278,039
5	585,610	297,917	287,693
6	539,060	275,473	263,587
7	551,677	283,488	268,189
8	597,844	306,275	291,569
9	461,659	241,264	220,395
10	550,412	288,878	261,534
11	331,852	179,463	152,389
12	545,417	299,631	245,786

Source: Central Statistical Organization (CSO).

There are several irregularities in this age structure and it does not look like a smooth population pyramid. The CSO realized the need to smooth the age groups, before using it as a baseline age structure for projections. In particular, the 5-9 age group was considered to be too large, relatively to the 0-4 and 10-14 year olds. There is, however, no basis for reducing the 5-9 year olds, as the ad joining ages show no evidence of age misplacement into the 5-9 year age group (Annex Table 19).

There is also evidence for undercounts among the 0-4 year olds (especially 1 year olds). However, the adjustments needed are not nearly as large as produced by the smoothing procedure used by the CSO, which produced a 0-4 year old cohort that is larger than the 5-9 year cohort. The data published in the CSO census report and in the Statistical Yearbooks did not adjust the single year age structure first, but created five-year age groups by adding up single years without adjustments. That is a relatively minor error, as preference for ages ending in 5 is about the same as preference for ages ending in 0. If preference for ages ending in 0 is greater than for ages ending in 5, this approach would cause more serious errors. The resulting age structure is shown in Annex Table 20.

ANNEX TABLE 20: YEMEN POPULATION STRUCTURE BY AGE AND SEX

Age	Total	Males	Females
Total	14,587,807	7,473,540	7,114,267
0-4	2,394,972	1,215,809	1,179,163
5-9	2,735,850	1,404,417	1,331,433
10-14	2,202,884	1,186,231	1,016,653
15-19	1,486,755	785,127	701,628
20-24	990,006	514,157	475,849
25-29	914,142	433,650	480,492
30-34	780,524	370,666	409,858
35-39	739,189	357,761	381,428
40-44	534,930	267,057	267,873
45-49	414,427	212,507	201,920
50-54	383,799	193,636	190,163
55-59	207,589	109,372	98,217
60-64	284,731	149,934	134,797
65-69	134,878	72,661	62,217
70-74	171,999	89,830	82,169
75-79	63,288	34,421	28,867
80-84	80,755	40,421	40,334
85+	66,040	35,095	30,945

Source: World Bank Staff estimates.

The World Bank population estimates and projections utilize data from the 1997 DHS. The change in fertility measured in the DHS is consistent with the increase in contraceptive use, and given the size of the sample (over 14,000 women, twice the size of the previous survey) is therefore likely to be reliable. There is always a possibility that the 1997 survey results were not correct due to errors in sampling or processing. No more information about this issue is available and internally the data are consistent (for example, the increase in contraceptive use and the decline in fertility). The change in the age pattern of fertility is also consistent with typical onset of the transition to lower fertility. The 1997 DHS measured an average fertility for the period 1992-97 that was about 1.0 child below the 1992 DHS. The assumption made in demographic projections is generally that such a trend continues in the future.

The Bank's projection below is a standard "cohort-component" projection as described above. The main assumptions are that fertility will continue to decline, and eventually reach "replacement level" of about 2 (when this is assumed to happen has no effect on the projection for several decades), and a continued decline in mortality. The assumed patterns in fertility and mortality, which are derived from model patterns, are shown at the bottom of Annex Table 21.

While there have been discussions among the Bank and the GoY (particularly MoPD and MoPH) on the differences in the estimates for population growth rate, these discussion did not lead to consensus so far. However, the issue will be addressed in the future and the Bank will collaborate with the GoY in conducting the next rounds of the population census and the DHS. These forthcoming surveys will help reaching consensus on the estimates in the future.

ANNEX TABLE 21: POPULATION PROJECTIONS FOR YEMEN

AGE GROUP	1995	2000	2005	2010	2015	2020
Total Males and Females	15272	17351	19858	22644	5514	28281
Males	7821	8851	10107	11510	12957	14355
0-4	1281	1464	1653	1803	1870	1847
5-9	1478	1226	1413	1605	1761	1831
10-14	1249	1457	1211	1399	1591	1747
15-19	855	1228	1436	1196	1383	1575
20-24	549	826	1199	1408	1173	1360
25-29	454	518	798	1168	1374	1148
30-34	395	425	496	774	1138	1343
35-39	367	371	407	479	751	1107
40-44	269	346	354	390	461	725
45-49	221	252	327	336	372	441
50-54	180	204	235	306	315	349
55-59	127	163	186	214	279	289
60-64	136	111	142	163	187	246
65-69	80	112	91	117	134	155
70-74	78	60	84	68	88	101
75+	102	88	75	84	80	91
Females	7449	8500	9750	11133	12555	13926
0-4	1240	1420	1601	1745	1808	1785
5-9	1409	1189	1374	1559	1709	1775
10-14	1069	1388	1174	1360	1546	1697
15-19	777	1049	1366	1159	1344	1530
20-24	509	752	1023	1338	1137	1322
25-29	500	486	729	996	1306	1112
30-34	436	478	469	707	969	1274
35-39	386	416	459	453	685	942
40-44	268	368	399	442	437	663
45-49	211	254	352	382	424	420
50-54	175	198	240	333	362	403
55-59	114	161	183	222	309	338
60-64	121	102	144	164	200	279
65-69	70	102	86	122	140	172
70-74	70	54	79	67	95	111
75+	94	83	72	84	84	103
Birth Rate	40	38.9	36.7	33.1	29.1	
Death Rate	12.6	11.2	10.1	9.1	8.4	
Rate of Natural Increase.	2.74	2.78	2.66	2.4	2.07	
Net Migration Rate	-1.8	-0.8	-0.4	-0.2	-0.1	
Growth Rate	2.55	2.7	2.63	2.39	2.06	
Total Fertility	6.400	5.550	4.700	3.988	3.434	

Source: World Bank Staff projections.

The GoY continues to accord high population growth rates a priority in its development plans and would like to attract greater support for family planning efforts. The decline in fertility to 6.7 during 1992-97 (and likely lower now), however, does not mean less emphasis on the importance of reproductive health. A population growth rate of 2.7% is still very high by all standards, implying a doubling of the population in about 25 years. Improving access to reproductive health therefore remains a critically important development issue in Yemen.

BIBLIOGRAPHY

Al-Sabbry, Mohammed. (2001). *"Development of Manufacturing in Yemen"*. Background paper prepared for the Study, World Bank Office in Sana'a.

Auty, Richard. (2002). *"Best Practices in Diversification for Mineral Exporting Countries"*. World Bank Managing Volatility Thematic Group Presentation.

Banerji, Arup and Caralee McLiesh. (2002). *"Sizing Up: Governance and the Business Environment in Yemen"*. Draft Report on the 2001 Private Sector Survey in Yemen, World Bank.

Barrès, Jean-François. (2001). *"Sources of Growth in Agriculture and Fisheries"*. Background paper prepared for the Study and the PRSP, World Bank Office in Sana'a, December 2001.

Brizzi, Gianni. (2001). *"Tourism Development in Yemen"*. Background paper prepared for the Study, World Bank Office in Sana'a.

CSO (Central Statistical Organization). (2000). "The Industrial Survey: 1999 Update". Sana'a, Yemen.

CSO (Central Statistical Organization). (various issues). "Annual Statistical Yearbook". Sana'a, Yemen.

Dasgupta, Dipak; Jennifer Keller, and Thirumalai Sirivasan. (2001). *"Reform and Elusive Growth in the Middle East --- What Has Happened in the 1990s"*. Paper presented at the Middle East Economic Association (MEEA) Conference on Global Change and Regional Integration: the Redrawing of Economic Boundaries in the Middle East and North Africa; 20-22 July 2001, London.

Deverjan, Shnatayanan; Williams Easterly, and Howard Pack. (2000). *"Is Investment in Africa Too Low or Too High? Macro and Micro-Evidence"*. Policy Research Working Paper, the World Bank, Washington D.C.

Devlin, Julia. (2001). *"Private Sector Environment in Yemen"*. Background paper prepared for the Study, World Bank Office in Sana'a

Easterly, William. (1997). *"The Ghost of Financing Gap: How the Harrod-Domar Growth Model Still Haunts Development Economics"*. Policy Research Working Paper, World Bank, Washington D.C.

FIAS (Foreign Investment Advisory Service). (1997). *"Yemen: Investors' Perceptions and Diagnosis of the Environment for Foreign Investment"*. World Bank, Washington D.C.

Gelb, Alan. (1988). *"Windfalls Gains: Blessing or Curse?"*. New York: Oxford University Press.

Johnson, Simon; Daniel Kaufmann, and Pablo Zoido-Lobaton. (1999). *"Corruption, Public Finance and the Unofficial Economy"*. Policy Research Working Paper No. 2169, World Bank, Washington D.C.

Kaufmann, Daniel; Arat Kraay, and Pablo Zoido-Lobaton. (1999 a). *"Aggregating Governance Indicators"*. Policy Research Working Paper No. 2195, World Bank, Washington D.C.

_____ (1999 b). *"Governance Matters"*. Policy Research Working Paper No. 2196, World Bank, Washington D.C.

IMF. (2001). *"Republic of Yemen: From Unification To Economic Reform: Yemen in the 1990s"*. Staff Report of the International Monetary Fund: 15 February 2001.

Rhee, Yung Whee; Katharina Katterbach, and Janette White, Janette (1998) *"Free Trade Zones in Export Strategies"*. Industry & Energy Department Working Paper No. 36, The World Bank.
SFYP (Second Five-Year Plan). (2001). *"Second Five Year Plan for Economic and Social Development (2001-2005)"*. Republic of Yemen, Ministry of Planning and Development, Sana'a.

Shawa, Alaédeen. (2001). *"Aden Urban Development Program: Assessment of the Institutional Framework for Private Sector Development"*. The World Bank.

Sherwood, Elisabeth. (2002.) *"The State of Manufacturing and Manufacturing Enterprises in Yemen: Causes, Prospects, and Remedies"*. Background paper prepared for the Study, World Bank Office in Sana'a.

Someya, Masakazu. (2001). *"Yemen External Competitiveness"*. Background paper prepared for the Study, World Bank Office in Sana'a.

Tanzi, Vito and Hamid Davoodi. (1997). *"Corruption, Public Investment, and Growth"*. IMF Working Paper No. WP/97/139, Fiscal Affairs Department, International Monetary Fund, Washington D.C.

World Bank. (1976). *"Memorandum of Economic Position and Prospects of the People's Democratic Republic of Yemen"*. Report No. 1231a-YDR; Washington D.C.

_____ . (1984). *"People's Democratic Republic of Yemen: Special Economic Report: Mid-Term Review of the Second Five Year Plan, 1981-1985"*. Report No. 4726-YDR ; Washington D.C.

_____ . (1989). *"Yemen: Country Economic Memorandum: Agenda for Sustainable Growth During the Oil Era"*. World Bank, Washington D.C.

_____ . (1995). "World Development Report 1995: Workers in An Integrated World". New York: Oxford University Press.

_____ . (1996). *"Report and Recommendation of the President of the International Development Association to the Executive Directors on Proposed Credit of SDR 53.7 Million (US$ 80 Million Equivalent) to the Republic of Yemen for An Economic Recovery Credit"* Report No. P-6817-YEM: Washington D.C.

_____ . (1997). *"Yemen: Towards A Water Strategy: An Agenda for Action"*. Report No. 15718-YEM; Washington D.C.

_____ . (1999). *"Republic of Yemen: Fisheries Sector Strategy Note"*. Report No. 19288-YEM, Middle East and North Africa Region, World Bank: Washington D.C..

_____ . (2000). *"World Development Report 2000/2001: Attacking Poverty"*. New York: Oxford University Press.

_____ . (2001 a). *"Yemen: Country Assistance Evaluation"*. Operations Evaluation Department, Report No. 21787; Washington D.C.

_____ . (2001 b). *"Yemen's Budget and Institutional Reform: Public Expenditure Review in Support of the Five-Year Plan"*. Technical Report, Middle East and North Africa Region, World Bank, Washington D.C.

_____ . (2002). *"World Development Report 2002: Building Institutions for Markets"*. New York: Oxford University Press.